Structure, Power, and Results

How to Organize Your Company for Optimum Performance

Structure, Power, and Results

How to Organize Your Company for Optimum Performance

WALTER R. MAHLER, Ph.D.

President, Mahler Associates, Inc.

 1975

Dow Jones-Irwin, Inc.   Homewood, Illinois 60430

First Printing, April 1975

ISBN 0-87094-093-7
Library of Congress Catalog Card No. 74–25815
Printed in the United States of America

To two well organized personalities,
SANDY and KENT

To JOHN P. ROCHE who gave me my first
organization planning assignment.

W. R. M.

Preface

Organizations evolve and change. They usually increase in size. Some fail. Some are acquired by others. As this evolution takes place one can be sure that structure is changed. The structural change may be an improvisation to take care of an immediate need. It may be a "follow the leader" response. It may be a well reasoned decision.

The importance of structural change is attested by the millions of dollars spent annually by business, industry and government for organization studies conducted by management consultants. Its importance is also revealed by the attention given this subject in the literature. All books on general management deal with the subject. Periodically, an entire book is devoted to organization planning. The major periodicals, such as the *Harvard Business Review*, have four or five articles a year on organization planning.

Interestingly, the generally accepted importance of organization planning has not led to any significant breakthroughs in methodology or theory. Venerable truisms on topics such as span of control and reporting to one boss are still bandied about. Some doubtful assumptions are propounded, such as the likelihood that "free form" structures will be more popular.

The National Industrial Conference Board and other groups frequently survey prevailing practices in organization structure. Occasionally a trend is noted, such as the trend to the Office of the President arrangement. By and large, the art of business organization has progressed very slightly since Henri Fayol, the French industrialist, first talked about organizational problems of manufacturing business around 1910.

A review of Peter Drucker's observations on organization structure in his most recent book, *Management* (1974), dramatizes this lack of progress. He presents five design principles. Two are old, and the three new principles aren't very revolutionary. Even more important, they aren't very helpful. However, Drucker does have some astute insights. He stresses that good organization structure will not just evolve. Organization design and structure requires thinking, analysis, and a systematic approach.

This book is intended to facilitate this thinking, analysis, and systematic approach. The phrase *behavioral approach to organization planning* is an accurate description of the philosophy of organization planning presented in this book.

It is my hope that the reader will find this book to be different from other books on organization planning. An initial difference is the book's definition of organization planning. I have found it helpful to subdivide this complex process into four segments: structure, power, job design, and staffing. I have also found it helpful to use certain processes for the analysis of each of these four segments and for design decisions as well.

It is my hope that this book will be helpful to executives faced with complex and challenging organizational design problems. I also hope it will be helpful to those individuals in staff positions who act as catalysts to get needed attention to organizational planning issues. The illustrations in this book have been drawn from business and industry. While I believe that the approach presented here is also relevant to governmental and nonprofit organizations, I have not provided illustrations to prove it.

A question might be raised as to whether this is a book on organization development. My answer would be that it is, in part. Three of the subjects stressed—structure, job design, and staffing—are best thought of as traditional management processes. The book's emphasis on power, however, is quite closely related to the concerns of those involved in organization development.

A word of appreciation is warranted to the hundreds of cooperative executives in a score of organizations who have patiently assisted in the evolution of the analysis and design processes reflected in this book. A special word of appreciation is due Mrs. Martha McNeil, whose well organized assistance includes extra duties, such as manuscript preparation.

A special contribution has been made by the constructive criticism provided by the participants in our Advanced Management Skills Program for General Managers. One week of the eight-week program is devoted to organization planning. The application efforts of the participants have provided much valuable feedback.

March 1975   WALTER R. MAHLER

Contents

part one
Introduction

Writers on organization planning cover the same subjects. They refer to the same traditional principles. The reader has a right to know from the very beginning whether this is another traditional book. I think it is not. Let me explain why I believe this to be the case.

First and foremost, this book stresses *process* rather than principle. Second, it subdivides organization planning into four distinct categories: structure, power, job design, and staffing. Third, it uses processes with each of the four categories to give a behavioral emphasis to organization planning. That emphasis should enable a planner to understand the way an organization behaves currently, to design a change leading to improved behavior, to make the change, and to secure the expected improved behavior.

It is too early to refer to the science of organization planning. Organization planning must still be considered an art. The above three unique aspects of this book are intended to take the mystery out of that art.

Chapter 1 explains the book's behavioral emphasis more fully and describes how it evolved. The behavioral approach of the author is then compared with the approach of other writers on organization planning. Finally, organization planning is identified as one of the basic processes of management. The others are planning, directing, controlling, and innovating.

In Chapter 2 the overall process approach to organization planning is outlined. A four-step process is presented. It can be applied to each of the four categories—structure, power, job design, and staffing. In this chapter, readers are encouraged to make a note of their current convictions about organization before going further.

1

A Behavioral Emphasis to
Organization Planning

Organization planning is something executives do and consultants and professors write about. Seldom has a business man written about organization planning. Years age, Chester Barnard[1] wrote a classic, *The Functions of an Executive.** He devoted several chapters to organization planning. Years later, Alfred P. Sloan[2] wrote *My Years with General Motors.* He devoted a sizable portion of the book to the evolution of the General Motors organization.

In 1956, Ralph Cordiner,[3] then President of General Electric, described his new decentralized organization in a series of McKinsey lectures, subsequently printed in a volume entitled *New Frontiers for Professional Managers.*

H. B. Maynard[4] talked a large number of operating executives into writing for his *Top Management Handbook* in 1967. Several chapters were devoted to organizational planning.

This brief summary about exhausts the literary contribution of operating executives.

---

* A bibliography—Part Eight—provides information on each of the references. These are listed in the sequence in which they are mentioned in the earlier parts of the book. A supplementary list of references is included for each part.

By and large, books and articles on organization planning are prepared by consultants and university professors. Two of the more prolific writers on the subject are Louis Allen[5] and Peter Drucker.[6] Other well-known writers on organization planning are Ernest Dale,[7] Harold Koontz and Cyril O'Donnell,[8] William Newman,[9] and Herbert A. Simon.[10]

In 1951, Paul Holden, Lounsbury Fish, and Herbert Smith[11] published *Top Management Organization and Control.* It surveyed the prevailing practices of top management in 31 large industrial companies in the United States. Twenty-five years later, a repeat survey of 15 large companies was made. Holden's new book, *Top Management,*[12] has an interesting chapter on *organization structure.* Here is one of its more provocative conclusions:

> During the past quarter century, probably no area of top management involvement has evoked more discussion, written or oral, than that of corporate organization structure. Students of the subject, both practical and theoretical, have expounded at untold length by the printed page and from the platform at countless meetings. What has been the result? The findings of this study lead unquestionably to the conclusion that structuring a company's organization is still a very practical matter, and the theorists as yet have made no appreciable impact.

This rather bleak pronouncement presents an interesting challenge to those who would write books about organization planning in the future. If their books are to have impact, then, evidently, they must differ from those which have been written in the past.

The author is bold enough to state that the approach to organization planning in this book is different. The major difference is a behavioral emphasis which contrasts with two prevailing approaches: the enunciation of principles and the reporting of surveys of prevailing practices.

This behavioral emphasis first appears in our definition of organization planning. We define organization planning as a systematic attempt to improve the performance of an organization by changing one or more of four elements: structure, power, job design, and position staffing.

The above definition applies to an established organization. This is, of course, the more frequently prevailing situation. For a completely new enterprise, the definition would be changed to read that organization planning is a systematic attempt to secure certain business results by providing for four key organizational elements: structure, power, job design, and position staffing.

This definition is quite unlike any found in the current literature. It may be helpful to review how the definition and this book came about. Some years ago, I was given the opportunity to conduct organizational studies. At that time I decided that it would be helpful to review the literature for ideas on how one actually went about doing an organizational study. I was looking for a process to follow in the conduct of such a study. I was then primarily concerned with questions of structure. A diligent search of the literature revealed only one suggested process. This process had to do with identifying work elements and building up from these to the entire hierarchy. A thorough study of this particular process led me to conclude that it was a rather limited one. Further, as I observed the processes by which organizations were actually studied by managers, it became clear that this was one process they never utilized.

The absence of a practical process for resolving questions of organization structure became a challenge. The challenge was approached from two angles. On the one hand, observations were made of the traditional processes being used by managers in many organizations. On the other hand, a search was made of the literature to glean suggestions, principles, or guidelines that might be helpful in developing a new process. One of the more frequent suggestions found in the literature was that an organization must be designed to accomplish objectives or purposes. This particular suggestion was found repeatedly in books about organization planning. However, a review of the actual processes, as they were carried out by typical managers, revealed that they seldom prepared objectives and seldom referred to objectives, even informally, when doing organization planning. It became apparent that managers often concerned themselves about a specific problem and that their efforts were aimed at setting up or modifying a structure in such a way as to enable them to deal with that one problem. This discovery led me to conclude that the structural process should begin with the identification of objectives or purposes. This is quite a contrast to the typical approach, which begins by drawing boxes to come up with a new chart. Further observation of managers, as they actually changed organization structure, led to the conclusion that their concern about problems had to be reflected in the process. Therefore, I decided that the second step, after establishing objectives, should be to identify obstacles to be overcome in achieving the objectives.

With further experience in the development of these two steps, it became apparent that questions about organizational structure had to be answered from the top down. That is, a given manager, whatever his particular level in an organization, must plan how the structure will help him to accomplish his objectives.

Further observation of managers in action led to the conclusion that they disagreed greatly about the relative merits of different types of structures. It became apparent that different managers were enthusiastic about different consequences of a given structure. This spurred further search of the literature. A very helpful concept was discovered having to do with the benefits that could be secured from a given structure. William Newman[13] refers to such structural benefits as the six key factors present in every organizational problem having to do with departmentation. The more one worked with these benefits, the more apparent it became that they were finite in number and that they could not all be accomplished at the same time. Experience in using the benefits with managers soon led me to conclude that they were quite helpful in resolving disagreements on a more rational basis. It also became apparent that the benefits really had to do with the way an organization behaved. In fact, in setting up a structure managers were really trying to get certain kinds of behavior to occur with some degree of regularity. I began to use the six structural benefits to encourage behavioral thinking about structure.

The next development in the evolution of this process was the observation that a large number of managers were enthusiastic about discovering and inventing new organizational alternatives. As one observed these efforts, it became apparent that there were only a few alternatives, but that these were being talked about in a different manner or being given different names as a way of selling changes. The same process seemed to be going on in the literature, with writers reporting with great excitement "new developments," which upon closer inspection turned out to be variations on old themes. A close review of the literature revealed a limited number of alternatives which appeared to be quite inclusive. This suggested another step in the structural process, namely, considering a limited variety of alternatives before making a change in an organization.

This is a reasonable account of the sequence of events that

led me to develop a process for thinking about structure, for thinking through to a new structure.

Another important evolution in my thinking took place as I began to work with structure. It became apparent to me that some frequently recurring problems in both actual operation situations and in the literature were not really structure problems. The more I dug into this, the more apparent it became that these problems were really power problems. In this case, the use of the term *power* is deliberate. It is a more inclusive term than the term *authority*. For example, a discussion about centralization versus decentralization really boils down to a discussion of how much power a central group will shift to operating groups. In large measure, the discussion about the necessity and importance of delegation is really a discussion of power.

It became apparent that one could think of power in much more deliberate terms than were usually employed. In one case, you could think of power in terms of differences in power across positions on the same level. This might be referred to as "horizontal power." In another case, you could think of the way power allocated at successive levels of an organization. This might be referred to as "vertical power." Power problems are frequently characterized by considerable conflict. In fact, this frequency of conflict has led some writers to refer to the importance of managing conflict as a critical element in dealing with questions of power.

My thinking about power and its importance was sharpened considerably by the stress the behavioral scientists placed upon questions of authority and the exercise of power. In addition, many other writers were beginning to discuss the importance of power and means for dealing with power problems.

Another step in the evolution of my thinking about organization planning had to do with the concept of job design. Again, my observations of operating managers, and my discussions with them, kept revealing that expected organizational improvements were not forthcoming when an individual had been appointed to a position because his responsibilities had not been clarified or his goals had not been established. During that same time, writers in the management field were giving increased attention to management by objectives and management by results. These writers emphasized the importance of defining positions in terms of responsibilities and results. Again, the twofold effect of observing managers in action and noting the emphasis of the management literature led me to develop yet another element of organization planning, namely, that of job design.

The final phase in the evolution of my thinking about organization planning took place as I identified situations in which a well-conceived new organization structure failed to work because an individual was appointed who was either unable or unwilling to do the job as it was designed. This phenomenon seemed to occur very frequently. Again, the writers in the field of management selection have always placed great stress on the importance of matching individuals with positions in order to get expected performance. This stress on the importance of staffing led me to identify the fourth critical element of organization planning, namely, that of staffing the newly designed organization.

Operating managers with whom I was working began to express appreciation for the help these four elements gave them in their thinking about organization planning. In fact, it soon became apparent to them that one of the reasons they were finding it difficult to do effective organization planning was that they were trying to deal with at least two and often all four of the elements at the same time. This seldom led to either sound analysis or sound decisions.

With this background information behind us, we can again consider our definition of organization planning. Organization planning is a systematic attempt to improve the performance of an organization by changing one or more of four elements: structure, power, job design, or position staffing.

The term *structure* has to do with the hierarchy of positions established for the organization. *Power* is defined as the ability to influence, to have an impact upon decisions and actions. An individual is considered to have power when he can make something happen. The concept as it will be discussed in this book is a much broader one than the concept of *authority*, the term usually employed. *Job design* refers to the establishment of a given position's responsibilities and the setting of goals against those responsibilities. The term *staffing* refers to the selection of an individual to fill a given position. Our definition makes it apparent that organization planning is but one management process. One can find numerous lists that include this and other processes in the literature on management.

However, management processes are usually said to include planning, organizing, leading, and controlling. Each of these processes is important. All are interdependent. It is impossible to determine which process is most important. It is also unnecessary. For a given organization, at a given period in time, one can always determine which process should be given priority when an effort is being made to achieve an improvement in performance. Those engaged in organization planning should be able to determine when a change in organization is the most appropriate action to be taken and when some other management process should be changed.

An effective organization planner must, first of all, be able to make an effective diagnostic analysis of the four major elements of an existing organization (structure, power, job design, staffing). The key to the effective planner's skill is the ability to understand just how and why an organization is behaving or performing the way it is. In addition, the effective organization planner can accurately anticipate how an organization will perform after changes in one or more of the four elements have been made. The effective planner must, then, be able to design appropriate improvements in one or more of the four elements. Finally, the effective planner must be able to implement the designs for securing the expected improvement in performance.

Notice that the above discussion of the effective organization planner did not mention knowledge of or the ability to apply organizational principles. Executives who have been faced with the necessity of making decisions about a specific organization report that there are few principles which have been helpful to them in their decision making. In this book very limited attention will be given to theorizing or the development of abstract principles. Rather, suggestions will be made for carrying out processes of diagnostic analysis involving each of the four elements of organization planning. These processes will be designed to enable an individual executive or a group of managers to think thoroughly and objectively in terms of each of the four elements. When we come to the challenge of design, processes for making design decisions involving each of the four elements will be suggested. The implementation of these suggestions can be done by an individual or a group.

To use a golfing analogy, the four elements of organization planning might be compared to the four critical elements of an effective golf swing, namely, grip, address, backswing, and downswing. If the would-be golfer develops a knowledge of the fundamentals for each of these elements, and then combines them into an integrated sequence of events, there is some likelihood that his performance will improve with practice. In the absence of this knowledge of the fundamentals, practice seldom makes perfect. The organization planner is in much the same position as the golfer. With a knowledge of the fundamentals, in this case the fundamentals of the processes to be carried out, subsequent practice and experience are quite likely to improve performance. In the absence of a knowledge of the fundamentals, a typical organizational planner is likely to be handicapped by a rather static level of ability as far as organization planning is concerned.

2

A Process Approach to Organization Planning

In Chapter 1 organization planning was defined as a systematic attempt to improve the performance of an organization by changing one or more of four elements: structure, power, job design, and staffing. There is value in a systematic process approach. The process to be suggested involves four steps:

1. Analysis.
2. Design or decision making.
3. Implementation.
4. Assessment.

This process can be applied to any one of the four elements. To deserve the designation *systematic*, organization planning should begin with analysis.

Organization planning, as we define it, can begin with an analysis of structure. That analysis may or may not lead to a change. Organization planning can also begin with an analysis of power. Here, again, a change may or may not be made. An analysis of the adequacy of current job design can also be a first step in organization planning. Finally, analysis of the performance of an incumbent can be a first step in organization planning.

The typical approach to organization planning taken by most companies is to concern themselves with structure or staffing. Usually, little attention is given to power or job design.

The Processes Covered in This Book

This book can be thought of as a "behavioral engineering" handbook. Part Two has to do with structure. Several chapters will be devoted to a process for analyzing an existing structure. Additional chapters will be devoted to a process for deciding upon a new structure. These processes have proven to be of value in enabling business executives to understand just how and why an organization is behaving or performing the way it is. They should also help executives to think through alternative structures and to anticipate accurately how an organization with a new structure will perform. Case studies have been included to illustrate how the processes work in practice.

Part Three concerns power. A chapter is devoted to methods of analyzing power problems in an existing organization. Several chapters are devoted to processes for making decisions on the allocation of power and its management. The emphasis is on processes which help the executive to understand how power is currently being managed and how improvements might be made in the way it is exercised. Also provided is a process for resolving the complicated power issues of a new structure.

Part Four deals with job design. A chapter is devoted to processes for analyzing job definition difficulties in existing organizations. Several chapters are devoted to processes for effective job design. Parkinson was absolutely right: work does expand to fill time. This means that jobs must be designed. The processes presented in Part IV are intended to help executives do just that, either as a means of improving the performance of existing organization or as a means of insuring the performance desired in a new structure.

Part Five, on staffing, considers processes for resolving staffing questions in existing organizations and a process for making staffing decisions for new organizational positions.

Part Six is devoted to follow-through. A chapter is devoted to processes for the implementation of organization changes in any of the four elements: structure, power, job design, or staffing. Another chapter is devoted to processes for the assessment of results.

Part Seven considers special issues. One chapter is devoted to organization planning at the chief executive level. An opportunity to study the stages in the evolution of organization structure and behavior in the construction industry provided the basis for the first chapter.

Who Should Do Organization Planning?

Before we get into the numerous processes involved in organization planning, it might be well to discuss just who should do organization planning. I would argue that organization planning is a prime responsibility of each executive. Further, it is a skill which each executive can and should master.

Let's consider the available options. Organization planning can be done by:

1. The top executive alone.
2. The top executive and his immediate staff.
3. A special internal task force.

4. An internal consultant or consulting group.
5. An outside consultant or consulting group.

Actually, several combinations of the above alternatives are often used. Consultants, either internal or external, or task forces may be able to make a contribution in the analysis step. They may also contribute in the design step. However, the critical decisions on changes must be made by the top executive. The top executive must be able to visualize the way the changes will affect subsequent organizational behavior. This requires in-depth thinking.

Our position is that the top executive must do organization planning. He should involve his immediate staff. He may find it helpful to involve other levels of management. And he can make use of such resources as internal or external consultants —but they should be "resources."

Where Should Organization Planning Start?

There is an ideal answer and a practical answer to this question. Ideally, the top executive should start organization planning, thus providing direction and guidelines on structure, power, job design, and staffing. Practically, it is often necessary for lower-level executives to proceed on their own because the·top executive, for whatever reason, doesn't want to be formal about organization planning. Consider the automotive industry. Because of the leadership provided by Sloan, General Motors has had a stability in structure and power which dates back to 1921. Neither Ford nor Chrysler have had this stability. While the dominant position of General Motors cannot be attributed to one or even a small number of factors, it is safe to conclude that over the years the stability of organization has been a definite advantage for General Motors.

In summary, there is a real value in accomplishing organization planning at the very top level of management. There is also a need for such planning at each subsequent level. However, a lower level can get more systematic about organization planning even though a higher level does not. Naturally, being systematic from the top down is the preferred situation.

Convictions about Organization Planning*

I have found it to be an interesting exercise to have executives make a list of their assumptions, beliefs, and convictions about organization planning. I call the list "Organization Planning ABCs." "A" stands for assumptions, "B" for beliefs, and "C" for convictions. Decisions usually evolve from strongly felt ABCs. We would encourage the reader to make a list of his or her current assumptions, beliefs, and convictions before reading further. Once the book has been finished and some of its processes tested in practical situations, the reader can come back to the initial set of ABCs. The ABCs should be in a constant state of maturing and improving.

Let me share two sets of convictions with you. One pertains to organization planning in general. The second pertains to organization planning as it now occurs in business and industry. You may find it interesting to compare your own lists with mine. These two sets of convictions provide a rather

---

* The use of pre- and postconvictions has proven to be a helpful device for executives who have completed our *Advanced Management Skills Program for General Managers*. This is an eight-week program, scheduled for one week a quarter for two years. In the program emphasis is placed upon learning and applying process skills, such as those stressed in this book. The participants, in effect, make a case study of their own organization. The set of postconvictions usually shows many significant changes. It is hoped that the use of pre- and postconvictions will do the same for readers of this book.

complete overview of the content of this book. They can serve as a preview and, subsequently, as a basis for review.

The Reader's Convictions about Effective Organization Planning in General

1.

2.

3.

4.

5.

6.

7.

8.

9.

10.

The Reader's Convictions about the
Effectiveness of Organization Planning in His
or Her Current Organization

1.

2.

3.

4.

5.

6.

7.

8.

9.

10.

The Author's Convictions about Effective Organization Planning in General

1. Organization planning is best thought of as a process for changing certain elements of an organization so as to improve the way that organization performs or behaves.

2. The four major elements of organization planning are structure, power, job design, and staffing.

3. Organization planning is not a science, but it is certainly more than an "art." Practice in organization planning, based on processes, should lead to significant improvement in an executive's ability to do organization planning.

4. An executive, who is an effective organization planner, can visualize how a change will affect the way an organization will perform in the future.

5. The structure selected should be the one which best facilitates achieving the organization's objectives.

6. Changes in structure are disruptive. Such changes should be made reluctantly.

7. Proper structure facilitates performance but does not guarantee successful performance. Improper structure leads to "doing it the hard way."

8. The most neglected aspect of organization planning is the allocation of power.

9. Most discussions of decentralization and line and staff are really discussions of power.

10. Personality factors have to be allowed for in organizational planning decisions. This is particularly true for top power figures. However, "bastardizing" sound structural decisions for personnel reasons should be done only after a thorough analysis of positives and negatives.

11. There are a limited number (seven) of basic structural alternatives.
12. There are a limited number (six) of basic benefits to be gained by proper structure.
13. All the structural benefits cannot be gained at the same time. Trade-offs are needed to get the optimum balance of benefits.
14. The trade-offs made to achieve this balance must be based on the organization's objectives and on the obstacles to their achievement.
15. The traditional organizational principles (span of control, one boss, etc.) are really not helpful in the process of organization planning because they do not enable one to foresee how an organization will perform.
16. It is helpful to define the responsibilities of a position; it is even more helpful to "attach" goals to these responsibilities.
17. Parkinson was absolutely right: work expands to fill time. This means that jobs must be designed and that the job design must be forced where necessary.
18. It is advantageous to involve in organization planning individuals who are going to be vitally affected by it. However, the top executive must make the final decisions.
19. Proper staffing is critical to the success of a revised structure. Improper staffing frequently vitiates sound structure.
20. A staff group can and should make a contribution to organization planning.

The Author's Convictions about Current Organization Planning in Business and Industry

1. Structural changes are made much too frequently.
2. New structures are introduced with much fanfare about

their advantages. However, little consideration is given to their disadvantages, and the new structures seldom live up to the announced expectations.

3. Changes in structure tend to be based on fad or "follow the leader" considerations rather than on thorough analysis.

4. Structural changes are often made when the appropriate action would be to remove a nonperformer.

5. The personnel function has not made a significant contribution to organization planning in the past, but it can and should make a substantial contribution in the future.

6. Greater use should be made of sub- or mini-business arrangements and matrix-type organizations.

7. Little or no effort is given to defining the jobs of higher-level executives. This is particularly true for positions in the office of the chief executive.

8. Improper staffing has led to poor results more often than has improper structure.

9. More attention needs to be paid to power problems and job design problems.

10. Size isn't too helpful a gauge for deciding when to shift from function to product.

11. Organizational changes should not be allowed without a thorough study and higher-level approval.

12. It is extremely difficult for large divisionalized companies to recognize that they can and should change the headquarters role. This usually means a small headquarters group and major business components, each with its own president and its own staff and operating units.

13. Because of pooled sales components, internal raw material sourcing, and other such "contaminations,"

"neat," "sanitary" profit centers exist in only a few situations.

14. Personalities play a major role in structural changes. This isn't all bad.

15. When managers move to another organization they impose their "old" structure on the new organization whether or not it is relevant.

part two
Structure

The importance of structure becomes apparent when one reviews definitions of organization planning. With rare exception, the definitions are limited to structural considerations.

Louis Allen* defines organization as

> the process of identifying and grouping the work to be performed, defining and delegating responsibility and authority, and establishing relationships for the purpose of enabling people to work most effectively together in accomplishing objectives.[1]

Alvin Brown, an early authority on organization, states:

> Organization defines the part which each member of an enterprise is expected to perform and the relations between such members, to the end that their concerted endeavor shall be most effective for the purpose of the enterprise.[2]

Allen has this to say about the importance of organization:

> Sound organization can contribute greatly to the continuity and success of the enterprise. . . . A properly designed and

___
* See bibliography for details on each reference.

balanced organization facilitates both management and operation of the enterprise; inadequate organization may not only discourage but actually preclude effective administration. . . . The manner in which the total work is divided and grouped into organizational units may directly affect operating results. . . . Overload, which directly affects operating efficiencies, may stem from poor organization. . . . Poor organization often results in waste motion and expensive overlap in work. . . . Sound organization facilitates delegation. . . . The organization structure is the framework within which the company grows. Expansion and diversification can proceed no further than the organization structure permits. . . . The organization structure can profoundly affect the people of the company, their morale and productivity. . . . The organization structure may have a strong influence on the development of managers. . . . Sound organization stimulates independent, creative thinking and initiative by providing well-defined areas of work with broad latitude for the development of new and improved ways of doing things. Properly conceived, the organization structure will demand creative results from creative people.[3]

The importance of structure is reflected in the billings of large consulting firms such as McKinsey; Booz, Allen & Hamilton; and Cresap, McCormick & Paget. A sizable portion of their annual billings comes from organizational studies.

The importance of structure is well illustrated by the skeletal structure of the human body. A person's skeletal structure may make jumping or running relatively easy or quite difficult. Occasionally, usually because of a deformity, a person's structure may prevent jumping or running. A seven-foot giant, such as Wilt Chamberlain, has a distinct advantage in basketball and volleyball, but his height doesn't prove very advantageous in many other sports, such as golf or tennis.

An organization's structure has an important influence

upon its behavior or performance. One type of structure will make it easy to get a certain type of performance; another type may make it difficult. Rarely does structure prevent behavior entirely. So while I might argue that structure is really quite important, I would prefer not to exaggerate its importance. If your organization has a less than optimum structure, you will find that behavior is inhibited. You will be doing things the hard way. The organization will be moving more slowly than it might. Achieving a given result will be more costly.

In Part II we will first consider a process for analyzing an existing structure. The aim of mastering the recommended four-step process is to develop the skill of analyzing an existing structure's behavior. Considerable attention will be given to six structural benefits. These benefits are, in a sense, windows to look through in analyzing how an organization is behaving. To facilitate mastery of the four-step process a case study will be presented.

Once the case study has been completed, we will take up the design of a new structure. Particular attention will be given to structural alternatives and their behavioral characteristics. Finally, several case studies of present and future organizational structures will be presented.

3

A Process for Analyzing
An Existing Structure

Do we have the right structure? Should we change our structure? These questions regarding structure are frequently raised by operating managers. Such questions become particularly perplexing when a major competitor makes a significant change in structure. Is this going to give him an advantage? Does he know something we don't?

Long observation of changes in structure being made in business and industry reveals four reasons for such changes:

1. To overcome one acute problem.
2. To copy some other organization.
3. To adapt to personalities.
4. To gain an advantage.

When an executive gets upset about a critical problem, such as the failure to achieve satisfactory financial results, he often considers changing structure or changing executives. As often as not, the structure gets changed.

Probably more organizational changes have been made in General Motors' name than in that of any other company. This isn't General Motors' fault. It's just that companies go around saying, "We are the General Motors of our industry." They then decide that they must set up an organization structure which they assume is like that of General Motors.

Adapting a structure to personalities usually involves restricting or modifying the structure to minimize an executive's weakness. Occasionally, however, a structural change is made to capitalize upon a unique talent.

Finally, some executives will change a structure because they feel they will gain improved operating results thereby. This often happens when an executive moves into a new position. The executive brings along the structure with which he became familiar in his previous position.

It is quite possible that a change made for one of the above reasons is right. It is also quite possible that it is wrong. Questions about change in structure can be best answered in terms of objectives to be achieved and obstacles to be overcome in achieving them. This leads me to suggest a process for analyzing structure.

A Process for Analyzing Structure

Let us again refer to the definition of organization planning as a systematic effort to improve performance by changing one or more of four elements. One of these elements is structure. The improved performance can be best defined in terms of objectives to be accomplished. A systematic approach is best accomplished by a process. A four-step process for analyzing the current structure has proven useful in deciding on questions about structure. The four-step process involves:

1. Establishing major business or operating objectives.
2. Identifying major obstacles.
3. Establishing needed structural benefits.
4. Analyzing current structure in terms of these benefits.

The value of this process needs to be emphasized before we get into the specifics on how to carry it out. The process helps to counteract the previously noted reasons for changing structure. The process assists executives in thinking about how the organization actually performs and the relation of this performance to its objectives. The process encourages the resolution of issues on the basis of two fundamentals:

1. Does the present structure help achieve objectives?
2. Does it help overcome obstacles?

It is quite possible that the present structure is optimum and that the organization's objectives are not being achieved for nonstructural reasons, such as inappropriate planning, leadership, or controlling. This means that a change in structure should not be made but that some other management process needs to be changed.

Step 1. Establishing Major Business or Operating Objectives

The objectives to be established are those of the top executive of the organization whose structure is being analyzed. The organization structure is, essentially, one means the top executive uses to get results. When analyzing the current structure, you are asking how well it serves the purposes of the top executive.

Some executives will have a well-formulated set of objectives. In that case, it is only necessary to select their major objectives and bring them up-to-date. Other executives do not have a formal set of objectives. In that case, these will have to be developed.

Entire books have been written on the preparation of objectives. Such extensive treatment is not possible here. However, the following suggestions will help in establishing a useful set of objectives or in modifying an existing set of objectives to make them as useful as possible. The more of these suggestions which are implemented, the more useful will the set of objectives be for the process of analyzing the current structure.

The Objectives Must Reflect the Strongly Felt Convictions of the Top Executive. This is an easy suggestion to make but a most difficult one to achieve. Decisions about objectives define where one wants to go in the future. Uncertainties about the future quite often lead to tentative or timid objective setting. One keen observer has well stated that you can really tell whether you have a firm objective when the first sacrifice is required.

The Objectives Should Be Set Out for a Five-Year Period. The main value of longer-term objectives is their usefulness in achieving a structure which can endure for a long period of time. Working against longer-term objectives minimizes the tendency to select expedient organizational alternatives.

The Objectives Should Cover the More Important Responsibilities of the Top Executive. It is neither necessary nor desirable for objectives to be comprehensive. However, objectives of major consequence should be established. Objectives should be set for any condition likely to have an important influence upon the subsequent success of the organization under consideration. A checklist of possible objectives for a variety of executive positions is provided at the end of this chapter.

The Objectives Should Be Stated in Terms of End Results. To be most useful, objectives should be stated in terms of end results rather than in terms of activities, programs, projects, and tasks. Again, this is an easy recommendation to make, but a review of many lists of objectives shows that it is frequently violated.

The Objectives Should Be Stated as Precisely as Possible.
The term *precise* is used deliberately. It usually means that one strives to state objectives in numerical terms. However, there may be important objectives which do not lend themselves to numerical definition. Two obstacles to precision frequently occur. One is inertia. Getting additional precision requires effort. Another is attitudinal. An ambiguous objective may be considered desirable. However, the more precise an objective, the more useful it will be.

The Objectives Should Be Stated Separately. This makes for ease in use in the process of organization planning. A paragraph with a mixture of four or five objectives is an awkward reference tool.

The Objectives Should Be Challenging, Yet Achievable. How high is high? The problem of how difficult to make objectives is a persistent one. If the objectives are too easy, they lose motivational impact and endanger the organization's success. If they are too difficult, they also lose motivational impact. One of the reasons a newcomer often changes an organization is that he comes in with much higher objectives, thus necessitating a change in structure. This often leads to staffing changes as well.

Step 2. Identifying Major Obstacles

Structure is a tool the executive uses to get results. He sets up a structure to help him achieve his business objectives and to help him overcome obstacles to achieving those objectives. Step 2 requires being formal about identifying major obstacles. An obstacle is any condition, internal or external, deemed to have an important adverse effect on the achievement of business objectives. The condition may be either current or anticipated.

Consider the following suggestions for identifying major obstacles:

1. Don't restrict the list to those considered to have an impact upon structure. You can't always be sure whether or not a given condition really affects structure. In any case, the obstacle must be dealt with in one way or another.
2. List internal and external obstacles separately.
3. Restrict the list to the conditions which are believed to be of major consequence.
4. Be sure to give thorough consideration to obstacles which may become critical in the future.
5. State the obstacles one at a time and in a brief, precise manner.
6. Do not endeavor to set obstacles for each objective.

The identification of obstacles can be done by the executive himself, by those reporting to him, by a task force, or by a consultant. It can range from an "armchair" approach to an intensive, in-depth study of both internal and external conditions.

Step 3. Establishing Needed Structural Benefits

Structural benefits represent the contributions the top executive can get from a given structure. These benefits reflect the behavior of a given structural alternative. A list of structural benefits will help in analyzing a current structure and in anticipating how a changed structure will perform. A list of needed benefits will permit identifying the advantages and disadvantages of a given structural alternative.

The list of needed benefits is useful in another way. It defines what any executive should expect from the organization structure. This means that the executive can then identify those things which will not be improved by a change in structure but will require action in the other processes of managing.

As further consideration is given to each benefit, it will become apparent that most executives have made use of these benefits in the past. The challenge is to use them as a part of the recommended four-step process and to do so skillfully.

Mastering the four-step process is mastering a skill—the skill of analyzing organization structure. As in learning any skill, mastering the fundamentals makes for a bit of awkwardness. The process we will suggest endeavors to help an executive to identify the benefits needed in light of his objectives and obstacles, and to do so without getting too complicated. It will soon become apparent that the needed benefits cannot all be achieved fully. Some vary inversely with each other. For example, an increase in specialization will mean increased costs and increased difficulties with coordination. Trade-offs across benefits will be necessary. Making these trade-offs will be the critical skill to be developed—the ability to secure an optimum amount of the benefits. A description of each benefit will be provided in Chapter 5.

Step 4 involves analyzing the current structure in terms of the benefits considered necessary. Suggestions for completing this step will be given in Chapter 5.

A checklist of possible objectives for five positions follows.

Checklist of Possible Objectives

Profit-Center Responsibility (General Manager)

1. Volume of sales. (Total? Percent increase? Competition?)
2. Net profit before taxes. (On net worth? On net sales?)
3. Other financial measures. (Costs? Inventory?)

4. Product mix. (Major product lines. Percent of total?)
5. Percent of market. (By major product line where available.)
6. New markets entered.
7. Changes in distribution. (Size? Type? Location? Specialization?)
8. Manufacturing facilities. (Size? Location?)
9. Changes in manufacturing. (Methods? Costs? Performance?)
10. Changes in management. (Systems? Methods? Policies? Programs?)
11. Organization structure. (Number of major operating divisions? Changes in structure?)
12. Policy changes. (Personnel? Management?)
13. Personnel. (Number of managers? Number of technical personnel? Percent production to nonproduction?)

Employee Relations

1. Recruitment of personnel.
2. Development and training.
3. Employee motivation, productivity.
4. Changes affecting employees.
5. Continuity of critical talent.
6. Manpower utilization.
7. Manpower planning.
8. Compensation. (Equity? Motivation? Control? Understanding?)
9. Safety of employees.
10. Employee benefits.
11. Union relations.

Marketing Manager

1. Volume of sales. (Total? Percent increase? Re competition?)
2. Product mix. (Major product line percent of total?)
3. Marketing costs.
4. Percent of market. (By major product line where available.)
5. New products or product lines. (Services.)
6. New markets to enter.
7. Changes in distribution. (Size? Type? Location?)
8. Pricing policies. (Related policies.)
9. Organization. (Structure? Specialization?)
10. Personnel. (Number of managers? Number in direct selling? Skill shortages?)
11. Personnel policies.
12. Changes in administration or managing methods.

Manufacturing Manager

1. Production capacity. (Total? Capital required? New locations?)
2. Productivity.
3. Costs per unit. (Versus competition? Breakdown?)
4. Raw materials. (Sources? Costs? Quality? Ownership?)
5. Quality. (Versus competition? Level?)
6. Maintenance. (Costs? Programs?)

7. Materials handling. (Costs? Improvements?)
8. Equipment. (Methods? Layout? Improvements?)
9. Safety.
10. Organization structure.
11. Union relations. (Changes in relationships? Contract changes? Versus competition?)
12. Personnel. (Number by major category? Supervisor quality? Skill shortages? Attitude changes?)

Financial Manager

1. Financial data.
2. Information system. (Type? Management controls?)
3. Capital. (Requirements?)
4. Changes in equipment, methods.
5. Business and managerial decisions. (Contribution?)
6. Cost of function.
7. Financial community.
8. Administration. (Changes in structure? New skills? Scarce skills?)

Engineering Manager

1. New product development. (Specific products? Products completed pilot test? Schedules met? Budget results?)
2. Product improvements. (Number of products? Amount of costs reduced? Market needs met?)
3. Technical service. (Volume of service? Timeliness of source? Revenue generated? Customer reaction?)
4. Consultation service. (Requests fulfilled? Results of consultation?)
5. Capital projects. (Timeliness? Accuracy? Subsequent results?)
6. Administration. (Budgets? Plans? Records? Reports?)
7. Personnel resources. (Recruiting? Training? Compensation? Communications?)
8. Relationships. (External? Internal?)

4

Structural Benefits

Have you taken lessons to learn the fundamentals of golf, tennis, skiing, or other sports? You will remember that the initial process was frustrating. You felt awkward. It took some time for things to settle in a groove, for movements to be natural. Well, the same phenomena will occur as you master structural benefits. It will be awkward for a while. It will be frustrating. However, once you have mastered this way of dealing with organizational structure, you can think your way in and out of structural issues in any type of formal organization in which you find yourself.

You will need to develop an understanding of structural benefits and to get a "feel" for them. You can then deal with structural questions with confidence. The structure of an organization is best thought of as a *tool* the top manager uses in achieving objectives and overcoming obstacles. The previous steps in the process have established objectives and obstacles as a basic reference.

The question now is, What benefits can the top manager expect from structure? The structural benefits reflect the way an organization behaves or performs. Having a feel for these benefits will help you in analyzing the current behavior of the organization. It will also help you to anticipate how the organization will behave or perform should the structure be changed.

Fortunately, any of you who have made organizational changes have made use of some of these benefits. You may not have given them a precise name. You may have given them names different from the names we will use. But you have used some of these benefits. So the challenge now is to use all the benefits and to do this systematically and skillfully.

We face several interesting challenges in understanding how to use structural benefits. It will become apparent that the benefits cannot all be achieved in full. Trade-offs are a necessity. We will identify six basic structural benefits. The challenge in each case will be to derive the nature of the sub-benefits required in light of the objectives and the obstacles.

Knowing the six basic benefits is of value to a manager because the six benefits are inclusive. They represent what a manager can and should expect from a proper structure. Or, stated in the obverse, a manager should expect the structure to contribute only these six basic benefits.

Let's begin by identifying the six basic benefits, behavioral benefits if you will, and then go on to define each more fully. The six benefits are:

1. Specialization of effort.
2. Facilitation of control.
3. Aiding coordination.
4. Securing adequate management attention.
5. Facilitating the development, motivation, and retention of key personnel.
6. Achieving minimum costs.

Specialization of Effort

Specialization involves having one individual or one group concentrate upon a primary outcome or result. In effect, it involves "attaching" an individual or a group to an important objective or obstacle. It is the first and most important structural benefit, for it leads to getting the work done, which is essential in achieving objectives and overcoming obstacles.

Specialization leads to rather predictable behavior. Specialized individuals concentrate on their particular work, their particular reason for being. This concentration leads to competence in performance. Energies are focused; enthusiasms are focused. This focused effort leads to considerable egocentricity. The specialty is considered to be of critical importance. The drive to achieve may be so focused in specialized individuals and groups that they show little interest or concern for other components or for the success of the overall effort.

Determining how to use specialization correctly involves looking at the objectives and the obstacles and identifying the areas in which specialization is most needed. Once this has been done, the defined needs can be compared with the specialization provided by the current structure.

The most critical question is the nature of the specialty of those who report directly to the top manager. The term top manager is here meant to be the executive who heads the particular organizational component being analyzed. The more important for the component's success a given specialty is assumed to be, the more likely it is to report to the top manager.

Fortunately, as we shall see in Chapter 7, the top manager has six basic choices in deciding upon the specialization of those who report directly to him. Briefly, these six are function, product, customer, process, knowledge, and geography. A combination of two of these, usually called a matrix, can well be considered a seventh alternative.

Facilitation of Control

It is important to understand this structural benefit correctly. Facilitating control doesn't have to do with control systems. It has to do with setting up of the structure by the top manager so as to give him "control" over the achievement of desired results. That is, the expected results are forthcoming or a "self-correcting" reaction takes place.

For example, quality is a critical factor in the aircraft and pharmaceutical industries. So the top manager in these industries, to whom the marketing and manufacturing functions report, will also have a quality control component reporting directly to him. It is this quality control structure that gives the top manager insurance that the critical quality of the product will be attained.

Another structural device for facilitating control involves setting up parallel groups to facilitate comparisons and provide competition. The telephone subsidiaries of AT&T provide a good example of this parallelism. Indices can be established for every major function of the company's subsidiaries, for each subsidiary is doing the same type of work in its geographic area. Another structural device for facilitating control is the "audit" group, whose purpose is to insure that certain standards or specifications are met.

It is interesting to note that the span of control is directly related to this benefit. A short span facilitates close control, often leading to overcontrol. A long span does not facilitate control. It often leads to the establishment of positions for one or two individuals who report to the top manager and "assist" him with his control function.

In applying the "facilitation of control" criterion, it will be necessary to identify the areas in which control is most critical to the success of an organization. Then the current structure can be analyzed to see whether there are any structural omissions or, possibly, structural redundancies.

The establishment of groups to facilitate control needs to be done very carefully. A group may be expected to perform a control role and another quite dissimilar role. For example, a personnel group may be expected to exert control over grievance decisions made in various segments of an organization. At the same time, it may perform a service role in the medical function, or a catalyst role in safety.

Special control groups must be justified by the critical nature of the variances they are to prevent. The facilitation of control does conflict with two other structural benefits— achieving minimum costs and aiding coordination. Trade-offs become necessary to get an optimum result. In summary, a "specialized" group gets the work done; a "control" group helps get it done "right."

Aiding Coordination

The top manager in a given organization must be sure that the necessary coordination takes place. However, a structure best secures this benefit when coordination takes as little of the top manager's time as possible, when the smallest possible number of participants are involved, and when coordination is achieved in a timely manner and at the lowest possible level. Many a top manager is finally forced to recognize that a structure must be changed when coordination becomes difficult. Among the common symptoms of poor coordination are too many meetings, too slow decision making, ambiguity on accountability, and loss of competitive position.

Structural alternatives to aid in getting coordination include the creation of special coordinating positions. Product manager, project director, and program manager are typical titles of coordinating positions. In some instances an assistant manager position or an assistant-to position is established to aid coordination. Another frequent alternative is the use of a committee whose responsibilities include coordination.

The shift from a functional organization to a product-type organization is usually called divisionalization. One result of such a shift is the move of the coordinating task to a lower level to get more effective and timely reactions. In applying the coordination criterion, it will be necessary to identify where coordination takes place and who is involved. Questions of timeliness and effectiveness can then be raised.

Securing Adequate Management Attention

This benefit is a tricky one. An individual or a group is set up to insure that adequate management attention is given to a responsibility which might well be neglected. The individual is expected to perform a "gadfly" or "catalyst" role. He is expected to stimulate the necessary attention of the top manager and other managers to a given responsibility. A good example of such a position is that of the safety director. Others are the director of organization development and the public relations director.

It is important to differentiate between specialization and adequate attention. Setting up a group to do a specific job is getting the benefit of specialization. Setting up a group to stimulate managers to act rather than to do something themselves is getting the "management attention" benefit. Both groups require special knowledge and expertise. But one group uses knowledge to get work done, whereas the other uses knowledge to act as a catalyst in getting others to get work done. The more important the gadfly role is considered to be, the more likely are those who perform it to report to the top manager.

Efforts to secure the management attention benefit have led to a great proliferation of "staff" groups, often at multiple levels of an organization. It is of great value to all concerned when there are clear-cut indications of the extent to which a staff group is expected to provide the management attention benefit.

It is obvious that this benefit is secured at the expense of the minimum cost benefit. In applying the management attention criterion, it will be necessary to examine the objectives and obstacles and then to determine where management attention will be most needed. One must also assume that other management processes, such as planning, motivational, and control systems, are not adequate to the task of getting the desired result. This definition of need can then be contrasted with the means for getting management attention that are available in the present organization.

Facilitating the Development, Motivation, and Retention of Key Personnel

This structural benefit is becoming increasingly important. Setting up a structure involves setting up a series of positions. However, the objectives of the structure are achieved by the individuals who are in those positions. If one cannot attract personnel competent to do the job, or if good men are frequently lost, then a most logical organization structure may have to be reconsidered.

The development of future general managers has led some companies to set up "mini-businesses" to give younger men a chance to make small-scale trade-off decisions across functions. The group vice president position is often created in order to develop, motivate, and retain impatient executives. The assistant manager position is also used by some organizations primarily for its developmental benefit.

A word of caution is needed at this point. Companies often remove an executive from a position because of nonperformance. A special position is sometimes created for such an individual. If the work is "made work," this position is a phony. Some organizations get encumbered with such positions. This approach usually ends up by being a disservice to the reassigned executive and a "bastardization" of an otherwise well-conceived organization structure.

In applying the development, motivation, and retention criterion, it is necessary to determine where the more critical needs for development, motivation, and retention are. In this connection, it is best to think of positions as being filled by a series of individuals to avoid setting up a structure for a given individual only to have that individual move. The assessment of the current structure may turn up some omissions. It may also turn up some "POPOS." These are executives who have been "passed over and placed on the shelf." Such positions are obviously contrary to the minimum cost criterion.

Achieving Minimum Costs

This important structural benefit is placed last on purpose. Often structure is changed to achieve the one purpose of economy. It is possible that an analysis of a current organization will reveal an extra level of management or other unneeded positions. However, if one looks at structure as a tool to achieve objectives and overcome obstacles, then one seeks first to build a sound tool and second to do as economically as possible.

There are several types of costs to consider. One type is the administrative budget. This would include salaries, benefits, and office support expenses for positions. Another is the time and effort involved in getting coordination, maintaining control, and securing management attention. An increasingly critical cost is that of turnover of key personnel. Experienced personnel may quit and take their knowledge elsewhere. Costs are incurred in hiring and training replacements. Behavioral scientists are pointing to the costs of apathy, boredom, and antiestablishment attitudes. These may be generated, in part, by a faulty structural design.

Application of the minimum cost criterion requires that every position be justified. The need for locating a position at a given level must also be justified. The need for each level of supervision must be questioned. A unique contribution must result to justify each level of management.

Serious questions must also be raised about all "non-operating" positions and groups. An individual set up to get management attention may engage in "empire building." It is interesting to see how empire building groups that get started at lower levels then "worm" their way upward to higher and higher reporting relationships.

5

Case Study

A process for analyzing a current organizational structure was described in Chapter 3, and structural benefits were described in Chapter 4. In this chapter a specific case study will be presented to illustrate how the recommended structural planning processes can be applied. The case study concerns a major division of a large chemical manufacturing company.

The structure of the present organization is shown in the organization chart.

Step 1.   Establish Objectives for the Division

The major objectives for the division were set out ahead for five years. They are as follows:

1.   Increase sales volume 15 percent annually.
2.   Exceed the return on investment (ROI) standards set for all divisions (14 percent).
3.   Make a significant contribution to sales volume by introducing new products annually (5 percent).
4.   Achieve a significant annual reduction in unit costs; hold overhead costs to a minimum.

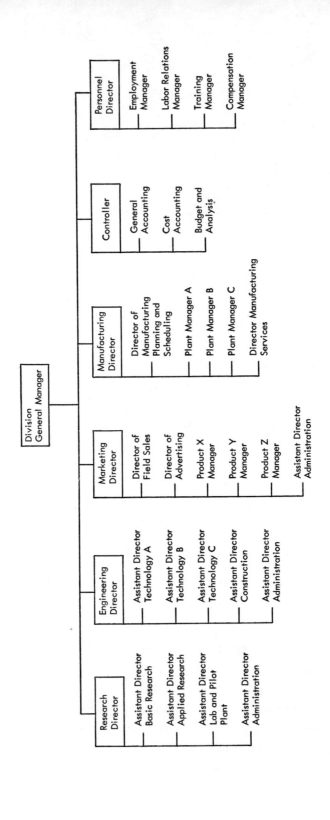

Division General Manager

Research Director
- Assistant Director Basic Research
- Assistant Director Applied Research
- Assistant Director Lab and Pilot Plant
- Assistant Director Administration

Engineering Director
- Assistant Director Technology A
- Assistant Director Technology B
- Assistant Director Technology C
- Assistant Director Construction
- Assistant Director Administration

Marketing Director
- Director of Field Sales
- Director of Advertising
- Product X Manager
- Product Y Manager
- Product Z Manager
- Assistant Director Administration

Manufacturing Director
- Director of Manufacturing Planning and Scheduling
- Plant Manager A
- Plant Manager B
- Plant Manager C
- Director Manufacturing Services

Controller
- General Accounting
- Cost Accounting
- Budget and Analysis

Personnel Director
- Employment Manager
- Labor Relations Manager
- Training Manager
- Compensation Manager

5. Acquire one new complementary organization at least every two years.
6. Professionalize management (methods, skills, etc.).
7. Achieve continuity of competent technical and managerial personnel.

More objectives were used in the actual case, but these selected objectives will illustrate the use of objectives as a first step.

Step 2. Identify Obstacles of the Division

The more important obstacles of the division were identified as follows:

1. Lack of a strong profit concern in the division except on the part of the General Manager.
2. Slow internal decision making across quite diverse products, markets, and intercompany relationships.
3. Serious lack of coordination across departments. The departments are major functional groups, such as Manufacturing and Marketing.
4. Absence of effective business and product planning.
5. Moving technology through research and engineering to on-stream production exceedingly slow.
6. Difficulty in cutting out weak product lines.
7. Development of personnel given lip service.
8. Heavy demand on General Manager's time for both outside and "upstairs" interactions.

Step 3. Establish Needed Structural Benefits

The third step involved identifying the structural benefits needed by the Division General Manager.

1. Specialization Benefit.   This benefit requires that a position or a group be established to achieve one or more objectives and overcome one or more obstacles. The Division General Manager will need positions:

   a.   To perform the major functions of Research and Development, Engineering, Manufacturing, Marketing, Controller, and Personnel.
   b.   To get the needed new products introduced annually.
   c.   To make the contemplated acquisitions. (This may not be a full-time position.)
   d.   To achieve a needed professionalization of management. (This may mean a change in the personnel functions rather than creating a new position or positions.)

2. Control Benefit.   The control benefit requires structural arrangements which provide for corrective action, preferably without the involvement of the General Manager. The most critical control need of the General Manager is control of profitability by major product lines. The multiple products subdivide into three rather natural groupings. The ROI objective is not now being met. Thus, control over product line profitability is critical.

   In addition, control over engineering products moving through the several technological groups is needed, in this instance by the Engineering Director. Tight control has to be exercised over indirect costs, such as administration, research, and selling. Unit costs of manufacturing must also be steadily reduced.

   A control benefit is now secured by the use of product managers versus the field selling organization. Similarly, in manufacturing a control benefit is secured by the use of central manufacturing planning and scheduling versus the various plant managers.

3. Coordination Benefit. The coordination benefit is critical. At the present time, trade-off decisions across functions have to be made for the three major product lines. Only the General Manager can do this. In addition, the large size of the organization makes it difficult for the functional directors to have the thorough knowledge needed for each of the product lines. The Marketing Director does have a product manager for each product line. Research and Development, Engineering, and Manufacturing do not.

Interaction with top corporate management, corporate staffs, and other operating divisions takes up a good deal of the General Manager's time. In addition, he requires considerable time for high-level customer contacts. The slow decision obstacle is due in part to the limited amount of time the General Manager has for coordination.

4. Adequate Attention Benefit. This benefit is usually secured by setting up a staff position to act as a catalyst in stimulating managers to give necessary attention to various issues. The primary needs reflected by the objectives and obstacles are:

a. Doing a better job of business and product planning.
b. Culling out weak products.
c. Attracting, developing, and retaining competent personnel.
d. Professionalizing management.
e. Increasing cost and profit consciousness.

5. Key Personnel Benefit. The structure can assist in attracting, developing, motivating, and retaining key personnel. In the present division, there is no position to help develop future generalists. In addition, there is no position to counter the natural egocentricity of the individual functions. Hence, getting needed team play or cooperation is dependent solely upon the General Manager.

There has been a lack of advancement for the functional directors. One, in particular, has been getting outside offers.

6. Minimal Costs Benefit. Achieving this benefit requires looking at such factors as unnecessary positions and excessively narrow or wide spans. It is also necessary to compare present costs with those that any alternative structure will entail. Consideration also needs to be given to costly situational factors, such as undue delays in getting decisions or lack of cooperative effort.

The above benefits can best be transferred to a worksheet in completing Step 4.

Step 4.   Analyze Current Structure versus the Structural Benefits

The structural benefits are convenient ways of identifying how the General Manager wants the organization to behave or perform. It is important to give greater priority to the critical benefits. These pertain to the most important objectives and the most serious obstacles. The critical benefits for this case have been italicized in the Step 4 Worksheet. What are the specific needs within each of the six structural benefits?

Step 4 Worksheet: Apply Organization Benefits

		Analysis:	
		Need Is Now Met by Position(s)	*Need Is Not Met by Position(s)*
1.	Specializing effort needed		
	a. *Major functional areas*	*a.* Six posi-	
	b. Acquisitions	tions	*b.* √
	c. Get new products to product revenue quickly		*c.* √
2.	Facilitating control needed		
	a. *On profitability of three major product lines*		*a.* Only by General Manager
	b. Engineering project control		*b.* Only by Engineering Manager
	c. Cost control—all functions		*c.* √
	d. Culling weak product lines		*d.* √
3.	Aiding coordination needed		
	a. *Across major functions for three product lines*		*a.* √
	b. "Upstairs" and interdivisionally	*b.* Only by General Manager	
	c. Across engineering on projects		*c.* √
	d. High-level customer contacts	*d.* Only by General Manager	
4.	Securing adequate attention needed		
	a. Developing personnel	*a.* Personnel	
	b. *Professionalizing management*		*b.* Not now done by Personnel
	c. *Increasing cost consciousness and profit concern*		*c.* Not now done by Controller
	d. *Business and product planning*		*d.* √
	e. Culling weak products		*e.* √
5.	Facilitating development, motivation, or retention of key personnel needed		
	a. Generalist position below General Manager		*a.* √

Step 4 Worksheet *Continued*

		Analysis:	
		Need Is Now Met by Position(s)	*Need Is Not Met by Position(s)*
b.	Position to counteract functional egocentric		b. √
c.	Mobility opportunity (status and responsibility		c. √
6. Cost minimization needed			
a.	Unnecessary positions	a. Not at three levels under consideration	
b.	Too narrow spans	b. None on present chart	
c.	Decision delays		c. Delays are becoming costly

Suggestions on Analyzing a Current Organization Structure

A four-step process for the analysis of a current organization has been presented. It begins with a three-level organization chart. The chart begins with the executive for whom the analysis is to be done. The analysis includes the next two levels. An entire organization can be analyzed by using the same process at successive lower levels.

Step 1 calls for a summary statement of major objectives. Step 2 calls for a listing of major obstacles. These are the objectives and obstacles of the executive who heads the structure being studied.

The remaining steps and the worksheet are designed to facilitate analysis of the current structure against the six basic benefits. Before undertaking the analysis, it is necessary to go from the generalized criteria to criteria adapted to the particular organization under study. As one reviews its objectives and obstacles, one asks, what specialization is needed? What control benefits might be needed? What coordination is needed? Where is management attention needed? Where is a concern about the development, motivation, and retention of key personnel needed? Specific answers to these questions permit analysis of the current structure for omissions. In the course of this analysis positions unrelated to needs may also show up.

Finally, the minimum cost criterion must be applied. By this time the justification for every position and every level of management should have been well established. Positions which have questionable justification need to be reviewed carefully. Note that the entire process applies to the two levels reporting to the top manager.

Planning for Several Levels

Once the above sequence has been completed for the top manager, the same process needs to be completed for each person reporting to the top manager in the new organization. This represents "terracing down."

Organization planning at the second level may lead to some changes in previous assumptions made for the total organization. However, these changes are not likely to be of major consequence if the planning for the top level was done in a thorough manner.

6

Designing a New Structure

In the previous chapter attention was given to a process for analyzing a current structure. Designing a new structure follows naturally from such an analysis. The analysis insures that the current organization is understood before it is changed. Occasionally, analysis of the current organization leads to a decision to leave it unchanged or to make minor modifications.

The analysis of the current organization involved establishing objectives, identifying obstacles, considering the general structural benefits, and establishing the specific needed benefits. The current structure was then analyzed against these specific benefits.

The process for designing a new structure involves the following steps:

1. Review the objectives, obstacles, and specific benefits prepared in the analysis of the current structure. Modify these where necessary.
2. Consider at least two alternative organizational structures. Plan for the two levels under the top manager.
3. Assess the alternative structures against the specific bene-

fits considered necessary. Arrive at a decision on structure which yields an optimum balance among the six
benefits.

The process for completing Step 3 is the same as that suggested in the previous chapter for analyzing the current organization structure. It will not, therefore, be necessary to
repeat the suggested process.

In effect, the decision on an organizational alternative is
a prediction that the benefits needed by the top manager will
be secured. This means that the structure is making an optimum contribution toward achieving objectives and overcoming obstacles. Don't let considerations of job design,
power problems, or staffing have an important impact at this
time. Your first task is to design a structure that will get the
needed work accomplished.

In the preceding chapter attention was given to objectives,
obstacles, and structural benefits. The critical new aspect
presented in this chapter involves getting a good grasp of organizational alternatives. Fortunately, these are limited in
number. Seven basic alternatives need to be understood. Each
has rather unique behavioral characteristics. Knowledge of
those characteristics permits the organization planner to
predict confidently the future performance of a new structure.
Designing a new structure is, in effect, deciding on needed
future behavior and selecting a structure that facilitates
getting this behavior. An inappropriate structure means that
the organization will get results the hard way.

The seven organizational alternatives are:

1. Function.
2. Product or service.
3. Customer.
4. Process.
5. Geographic.
6. Knowledge.
7. Matrix.

Organizational alternatives are really ways of grouping work. In deciding among these alternatives, the critical question is, who should report directly to the top manager. This determination influences the nature of the top manager's position and, of course, has an impact on the choice of alternatives at lower levels of the organization. With this question in mind, each of the seven basic organizational alternatives will be considered in considerable detail in the next chapter.

7

Structural Alternatives

Structural alternatives are different ways of grouping work. The alternative may refer to the nature of the work, such as a function of engineering or a process of assembly; the outcome of the work, such as a product; the recipient of the work, such as a customer; or the geographic location in which the work takes place.

The structural alternatives are:

1. Function.
2. Product.
3. Customer.
4. Process.
5. Knowledge.
6. Geographic.
7. Matrix.

As far as we can determine, these alternatives are inclusive. They certainly include the alternatives most frequently encountered. Each organization employs several of the alternatives.

As we noted earlier, the most critical question governing

selection of the structural alternative or alternatives is, who should report directly to the top manager. How this question is resolved governs the choice of alternatives at subsequent levels.

An analysis of the typical behavior in each structural alternative follows.

The Functional Alternative

Functional groups are typically found in manufacturing companies. Charts of functional organizations follow.

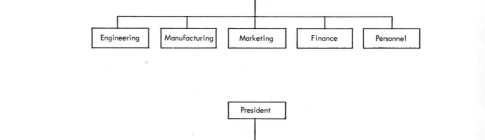

Characteristics of a Functional Organization

Let's look at how a functional organization behaves, from the viewpoint of the top manager in the organization. Each function concentrates on its own work. Each function's internal efficiency is likely to be high. As a function grows in size, it can begin to afford more specialization, which leads to greater efficiency in getting specific work done. Each function develops its own esprit de corps. Sometimes it begins to look upon other functions as the "enemy." Manufacturing, to be a bit extreme, is usually happiest when it can produce one product in large volume. This permits things to hum. Marketing is happiest when it can get each customer's unique preferences met on short notice. This natural egocentricity creates a potential for considerable friction.

The functional organization is likely to have more equipment, people, and other resources available within a given function. It can allocate and reallocate these resources with greater efficiency. For example, it can create more full-time specialized positions.

There is competition among functions for attention, privileges, resources, and advantageous decisions. "Jockeying for position" takes place. Each function is likely to be egocentric, sometimes highly egocentric. The various functions get concerned about doing their own thing. It is quite likely that the lower management levels are more egocentric than the higher levels. Friction and conflict between functions is common. Occasionally, sabotage takes place. The top manager wonders why grown men act like children. The fact that such behavior goes on year after year, reveals the influence of the functional environment on the behavior of individuals.

The top manager has to be involved in the coordination of all critical issues. It is unlikely that functions will be able to coordinate on their own, except on minor matters.

As the organization continues to grow, it becomes necessary for three levels of managers to get together to coordinate

Level 1		General Manager	
Level 2		Engineering Manager	Manufacturing Manager	Marketing Manager
	A {	Engineering Supervisor Product A	Manufacturing Supervisor Product A	Marketing Supervisor Product A
Level 3	B {	Engineering Supervisor Product B	Manufacturing Supervisor Product B	Marketing Supervisor Product B

At this point, coordination becomes time consuming. It has to be programmed out ahead. While the top manager is coordinating on Product A, any vital coordination of Product B has to wait. The delays become more prevalent as the number of products multiply. Quite often, representatives of the functions for a particular product or product group are set up as a "standing committee." One organization formed product group committees that included representatives of research, operations, sales, and engineering. Naturally, they were entitled the "Rose" committees.

Within a function, the entire hierarchy becomes quite responsive to the top functional manager. He has usually been "in the business" a long time. He is respected as a manager who knows the functional work. This makes his leadership role a natural one. Add to this the leadership required in "fighting" the other functional "enemies," and it becomes quite likely that a functional group will be cohesive.

The generalist view is certainly not developed. In spite of himself, each functional leader tends to be parochial in his views. Long experience in one function tends to "condition out" the entrepreneurial instincts needed in future general managers. When a functional manager becomes a general manager, he has to learn the other functions. It takes him some time to make his trade-off decisions in an objective manner. Some general managers never overcome their functional "inheritance." However, within the functional organization, at least the larger functions are likely to be taller from a structural viewpoint. This provides more upward mobility opportunities for functional personnel. The tendency is for functional men to remain in their initial function throughout their careers.

As the organization grows larger and its products and markets become more diverse, the top manager finds it difficult to maintain control. At this point, he often sets up a strong control group reporting directly to him. The most famous of these groups were the ones set up by General Somervell when he first came to the Koppers Company after World War II. The establishment of the control group leads to additional friction. The functional groups now have a common "enemy" and a basis for collaboration. Of course, the collaboration may not be in the interests of achieving overall objectives.

By their very nature, each of the functions has its own goals and objectives. These are often in conflict. For example, the quality control group may enforce high standards that handicap the production group. Rejects by the quality control group may lead to increased production costs and missed shipments.

In a functional organization profits tend to be of much greater concern to the top manager than to the functional managers. The marketing function fights for sales, manufacturing pushes for high production, engineering seeks technological leadership. The data which go to the various functions seldom provide a basis for real concern about profit results. Top managers often experiment with administrative procedures and reward systems that will get functional managers to be more "profit" oriented. These may help, but the functional structure basically inhibits genuine profit concern on the part of the functional managers.

It is quite likely that one function will dominate the others. Some companies are known as being engineering dominated, or marketing dominated, or finance dominated. In some situations, the dominance of a given function is justified by its relative contribution to the success of the enterprise. In many situations, the dominance of a function is due to differences in the strength of personalities. Unjustified dominance leads to behavior which sub-optimizes overall results.

Measurement of the results achieved by a given function and of a function's contribution to the overall success of an organization is difficult at best. Decisions of consequence are made by the top manager. The top manager has to be intimately involved in day-to-day operations. Behaviorally, one can readily predict that the pressure of short-term issues will leave the top manager little time or inclination to take up long-term issues.

For a variety of reasons, the functional organization has difficulty in diversifying into new product lines. The embryonic product line doesn't get the nurturing that is needed. "Old work" gets done, but "new work" doesn't! Consequently if the introduction of new products is required to sustain growth, growth slows down.

It may seem that the negatives have been overstressed in this description of the characteristics of a functional organization. The critical requirement is to give appropriate weighting to both positive and negative characteristics. This is best done in terms of structural benefits. As an organization begins to grow in size and in the complexity of its products and markets, the original functional organization begins to become dysfunctional. This leads to the consideration of other organizational alternatives.

The Product Alternative

In our discussion of the product organization, wherever the term *product* is used, it is to be understood as interchangeable with the term *services* for a service organization.

Charts of product-type organizations take various forms as shown in Examples A–D.

EXAMPLE A

A Product divisionalized Company

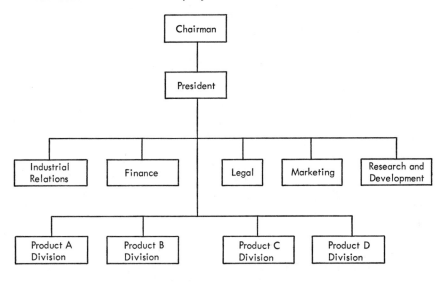

EXAMPLE B

Division Product Grouping

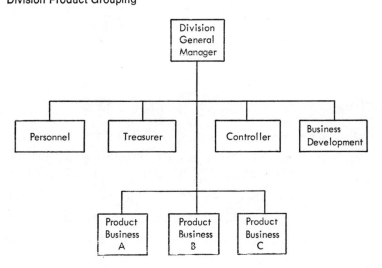

EXAMPLE C

Product.Grouping within a Function

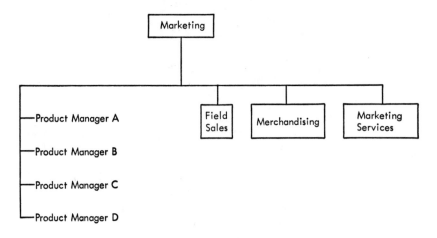

EXAMPLE D

A Service Grouping

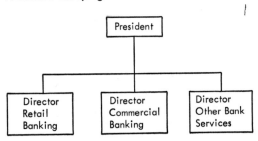

Characteristics of a Product-Type Organization

Product groups usually evolve from a functional organization. When "product" divisions are established, the process
is sometimes referred to as divisionalization. Product groups
have often been established within a functional group, such
as marketing. Let us first consider the characteristics of a
product division that reports to the company president. The
general manager of such a division usually has the basic

functions of marketing, manufacturing, engineering, finance and personnel reporting to him.

The behavior of a product division (or a service division) has the following characteristics. Division effort is concentrated on the growth and profitability of the assigned product (or service) line. The range of products (or services) in the line is restricted, so that coordination takes place much more readily. It also takes place at a lower level than it did in the former functional setup. This is true until the division outgrows itself. Then the behaviors of the displaced functional organization begin to recur.

Each product division drives for optimal financial results for itself. Each becomes very protective of its product line. Well, protective in a predictable way. It doesn't mind having another division take a nonprofitable line, a "dog," but it fights to the last to avoid losing a profitable line. So-called charter clashes occur with regularity.

Particularly when first established, divisions demand "freedom" and resent restrictions. They prefer to have their own resources. They prefer to be geographically separated from headquarters. Making the trade-off decisions, for example, between profit and growth becomes a challenge to the division general manager. Under the strong pressure which exists for short-term results, longer-term considerations are usually neglected. In extreme instances the subordination of long-term considerations to short-term results jeopardizes the future of a business; this is usually called "milking the business." The consequences are most readily recognized by the successor of the general manager who has made his mark and moved on.

When an organization shifts from a functional to a product arrangement, a major change occurs in the nature of the top manager's job. Let's assume that the organization making this shift is a company. The top manager's job changes drastically. For most top managers it comes as a shock to find that they can no longer make the trade-off decisions across functions. The top manager's attention is now turned to strategic planning, allocation of resources, and controlling the overall performance of divisions. Corporate policies and procedures become necessary. Corporate staff groups are set up or expanded to develop and install these policies and procedures. Divisions see such efforts as restrictive. Resentment builds up between the divisions and headquarters groups. Each side sees the other as lacking understanding, noncooperative, and not too effective.

The top manager is now faced with the difficulties of coordinating across divisions on such issues as purchasing, personnel, pricing, common customers, and public and governmental relations. Quite often confusion exists on the respective roles of headquarters "staff" groups and "divisional" staff groups. What is the split of responsibility, for example, between a corporate personnel group and a divisional personnel group? How does a corporate director of manufacturing relate to division manufacturing and to the general managers of divisions? Even when the confusions are removed, differences of opinion remain. In effect, corporate groups trying to insure the success of the total enterprise conflict with divisions which are almost exclusively interested in "doing their thing."

The major behavioral benefits of the product- or service-type organization begin to show up over a period of time. The organization is able to increase its volume of sales. It is able to increase, or at least to maintain, its profitability. Divisionalizing results in diversification so that all the eggs are not in one basket. Finally, the division general managers are getting generalist experience under fire. This increases the number of individuals with generalist background who may be available for eventual top general management assignments. Usually, the new division general managers are younger men. Getting generalist experience at an early age accelerates their development.

Decision making which involves trade-offs across functions now occurs at a level lower in the structure. Not surprisingly, in light of our previous discussion of functional organizations, decisions are now made more rapidly and, usually, with a "feel" for their impact on results. It is easier to bring in outsiders to head up a product division.

Predictably, establishing product groups results in higher administrative costs. It becomes difficult to move unique talent from one product group to another. Equipment and facilities are often duplicated. These are some readily apparent characteristics of a product-type organization structure.

The Customer Alternative

It is apparent that this organizational grouping is by a particular type of customer or market served. Top managers of large manufacturing companies seldom select this as the structure reporting directly to them. In such companies the customer alternative is more likely to be used by functions which are a level or two below that of the top manager, such as marketing. However, in service companies, such as banks, advertising agencies, and brokerage houses, the customer-type organization often reports directly to the top manager. Charts of several customer-type structures are shown in Example E–G.

EXAMPLE E

Customer-Type Reporting to a President

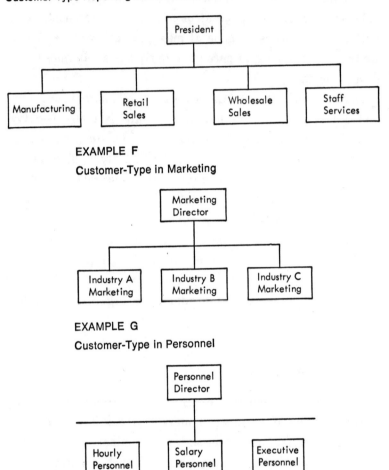

EXAMPLE F

Customer-Type in Marketing

EXAMPLE G

Customer-Type in Personnel

Characteristics of a Consumer-Type Organization

Whatever the level at which it is established, the customer-type organization has certain behavioral characteristics. It is very responsive to customer needs and demands. It becomes very knowledgeable about customers. A strong, often personal, link exists between the organization and the customer. The organization is likely to have a strong "service" emphasis. Often the customer-type organization is not too concerned about costs and profits. This leaves the top manager with "control" problems. Service is quite likely to be under control, but costs and profits are not. The problem of controlling costs and profits becomes even more interesting when the organization has difficulty in getting data on the costs of providing a given service to a customer.

Usually several customer groups and one or more supporting groups report to the top manager. This means that the top manager has to coordinate across these groups. Coordination of this type is likely to involve the allocation of resources and the arbitration of competing claims. Unless a scarcity exists this isn't likely to be a difficult task.

Real expertise is developed in a given industry or customer area. This becomes particularly relevant when the technology is high. The stress on the customer interferes with the development of generalists unless pressure is put behind transfers into different segments of the organization.

An interesting characteristic of customer-type organizations is the greater likelihood of losing good men who quit to join a customer.

The Process Alternative

This type of structure is characterized by the stages through which the work moves. Oil companies are sometimes referred to as process industries. A domestic oil company is likely to have the following organization.

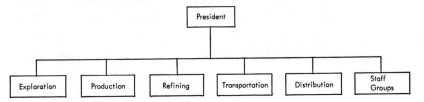

A head of manufacturing for a large airframe manufacturer might have the following reporting positions.

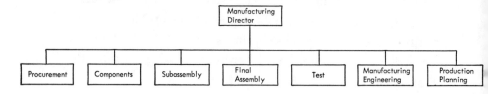

In addition to basic industries, transportation companies
can be considered process-type organizations. Shift-type organizations are often subdivisions by time of a continuous
process.

Characteristics of a Process-Type Organization

The characteristic behavior of process-type organizations
appears to be consistent no matter at what level the process
structure is found.

Each process group concentrates upon doing its thing. The
process groups become highly specialized and highly effi-
cient. Repetitive processes are standardized to insure efficiency. In many instances, the process is both "art" and
"science." Long experience and skill lead some process specialists to become recognized experts.

Timing is extremely important. Coordination along the
entire process is critical. The top manager has to have one
or more special groups to provide timely coordination across
all process groups.

Quality is a critical factor. If quality specifications are
not met at one stage, all subsequent stages get into trouble.
They may have to reprocess or return the product. Costs are
incurred and delays occur. In some instances, there is a complete shutdown. It is therefore safe to predict that friction between successive process groups will be frequent and that
"buck-passing" will become a high art. Groups at the end of

the process cycle usually feel victimized. They can be permitted a mild paranoia.

The top manager of a process-type organization is a busy man. He must make critical decisions on extremely tight schedules. Interruptions due to natural causes or changes in ultimate demand for the product require immediate, co-ordinated action by all process groups.

Long experience in one stage of a process doesn't develop the generalist ability required at the top. Often the top manager supports himself by having a specialist for each major process group.

It is extremely difficult to measure results in a process-type organization. The costs of a stage in the process can be derived, but not without many arbitrary decisions. The determination of value added for a given phase in the process is extremely difficult. Profitability can be determined only after the product has been delivered to the customer. This means that the top manager over process groups is the only one who has real control over profitability.

The Geographic Alternative

As is implied by its name, this type of structure is characterized by location. Multinational organizations are likely to have such structure.

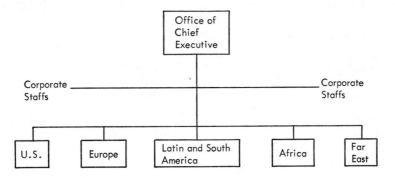

A field-selling organization is, of necessity, geographic.

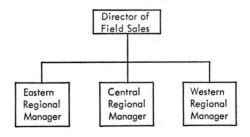

Service-type organizations often have a geographic structure after they expand from their original location. Banks, hotels, and utilities would exemplify geographic arrangements as noted below.

A bank might organize its national and international operations as follows.

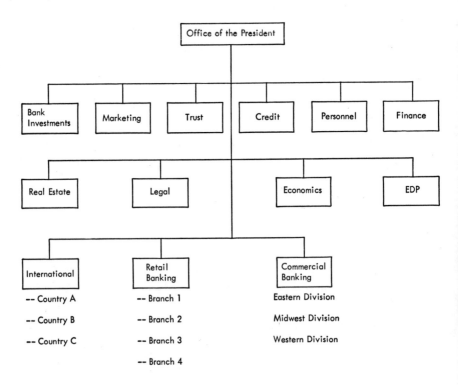

A national hotel chain might be organized along the following lines.

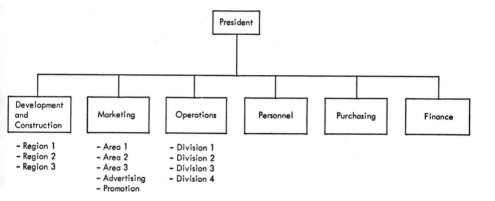

A utility with divisional operations at a number of different locations might adopt a structure organized along the following lines.

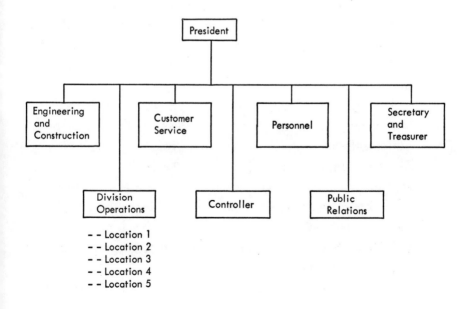

Characteristics of a Geographic Organization

What are the behavioral characteristics of geographic organizations? The "resident" managers learn the culture of their particular regions. They stress the unique features of their areas. In fact, they often overemphasize such features. This may be done to make it easier for the local regional group. Often it is done to insure that the central group take uniqueness into account.

Remoteness leads to a mild paranoia on the part of regional groups. They feel misunderstood, neglected, and unsupported. The central groups develop their own unique mannerisms. They usually see themselves as superior to the regions. They see the regions as resistant and uncooperative and as manifesting a "not invented here" attitude.

The regional groups often regard central support groups uncooperative and sometimes as ineffective. Such attitudes are often reciprocated by the central groups.

Regional groups build up particular hostility to the "visiting" routine. This is particularly so when visits seem to coincide with seasonal events or vacation plans. Visitors can't win. If they stay a short time, the hosts think they really aren't interested or helpful. If they stay a long time, the hosts think they are trying to overcontrol.

The primary value of the geographic organization to the top manager is its effectiveness in meeting the unique requirements for business success in a given geographic area. The top manager must depend upon the local manager for control. The local manager usually gets generalist experience.

An interesting problem occurs when customers have multi-locations but do purchasing on a centralized basis. This usually leads to a hybrid organization, part geographic and part customer-type.

The regions quite often fail to make full use of the staff

contributions of the central group. Regional costs tend to creep higher and higher. The same is true of central headquarters costs.

Usually each geographic component is quite autonomous. This makes it easy for the top manager to hold a region responsible for business results (profits, sales, costs, etc.). It may also give him the benefit of peer pressure, as each regional manager competes to excel the others.

When needed, coordination across geographic components is difficult to get. This problem requires the direct attention of the top manager. To solve it, he may need the assistance of one or more groups.

The Knowledge Alternative

The development of components oriented primarily around knowledge is relatively recent. Usually a few such components report to the top manager, along with one of the more traditional groupings already discussed. Examples of knowledge components are an economics department, a legal group, or a technology department designed to help top management make technical decisions.

Knowledge organizations are almost too recent to permit generalization about their behavioral characteristics. However, the following observations seem to be pertinent.

Individuals with knowledge are highly specialized. This specialization leads them to be very profound in their narrow areas. The interesting thing to note is their tendency to stray from these areas. Knowledge specialists often fancy themselves able to make the broad business decisions of their superiors rather than as mere sources of special insights and information. It might be added that top managers sometimes encourage such attitudes on the part of the knowledge specialist because they see the stands taken by the knowledge specialist as objective, in contrast to the advocacy stands of the other individuals who report to them.

As organizations become larger, they realize that one of their unique advantages is the ability to take on bigger opportunities. Such opportunities involve high-risk commitments extending over a period of many years. Today's decisions become critical to business success for several decades. Under such pressures, top managers begin to use knowledge specialists or groups to insure sound judgments on long-term commitments.

The Matrix Alternative

The matrix organization is often considered to be new. It really isn't. It has existed within marketing organizations for years, with the product manager and field sales as the two parameters. What is new is having the matrix report to a general manager or a president. The matrix organization became popular with large defense programs. It is now being used frequently by nondefense organizations.

FIGURE 1

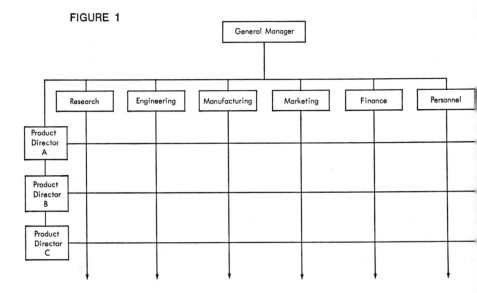

Let us consider several matrix organizations. Figure 1 shows a matrix organization that reports to a general manager. It will help if this particular matrix is explained. In the "pure" functional organization, the resources are maintained within the functional groups, such as engineering. In the "pure" product-type organization, the product directors are responsible for the business success of their respective product lines. This matrix gives the general manager the benefits of both a functional and a product-type organization. It is a compromise. It avoids the costs and some of the disadvantages incurred in shifting from a functional to a product division setup.

An example of a matrix that reports to a chief engineer is shown in Figure 2.

FIGURE 2

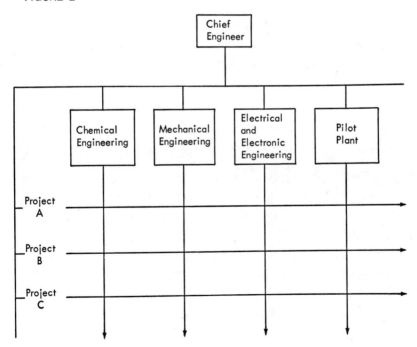

FIGURE 3

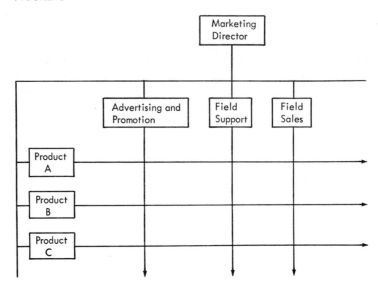

The example of matrix organization has to do with marketing. Figure 3 illustrates a product/function matrix. Other matrix possibilities include function/customer, function/geography, and product/geography. The same behavioral characteristics would prevail in all of these structures.

Characteristics of Matrix Organizations

Let us now consider the behavioral characteristics of matrix organizations.

1. Conflict is absolutely certain. It can't be avoided. However, conflict is a benefit of the matrix organization. That is, it is a benefit if the conflict is managed.

2. The top manager who understands the matrix setup usually likes it. On the other hand, those reporting to him are not likely to be pleased with this type of organization. The product directors dislike having responsibility without full

authority over the functions. The functions dislike having so many bosses. Neither the product directors nor the functions like the joint or shared responsibility aspects of the matrix organization. At least they don't until they have lived with these aspects successfully for a number of years.

3. The newly appointed product directors are likely to have functional background only. They are now in a generalist position. It takes several years for them to really become generalists. Some are not likely to make it.

4. The shared or joint responsibility of the matrix organization requires a high level of trust and confidence. It requires the ability to do timely problem solving. The leadership style of the top manager makes a great deal of difference here. If the top manager doesn't stimulate a high level of trust, then the unavoidable conflict of a matrix organization can't be managed effectively. Personality conflicts erupt, cliques form, defensive maneuvers abound, energy is diverted to "internecine warfare."

5. The product director side of the matrix almost always strives to "capture" its own resources by taking over one function and then another. If this process is unchecked, the functions are weakened and eventually emasculated. This usually requires a shift toward a product division setup. The opposite danger also exists. If functional groups are allowed to be impervious to the requirements of the product or project directors, then the potential benefits of the matrix for the product or project are not secured. The product or project directors get frustrated and quit. This leads either to a reversion to a straight functional organization or to a product divisionalization.

One can't predict how a given matrix organization will behave. The leadership style of the top manager is critically important. The potential benefit of the matrix organization is that it can give the optimum results one might expect from both a functional and a product setup. The negative possibility is disastrous, nonproductive conflict. The matrix organization is a tricky, delicately balanced structure. It must be managed effectively, or chaos results.

6. The matrix organization enables the top manager to coordinate and control more readily. Several positions are working full time on these two benefits for him. Consequently, the top manager can manage a matrix organization which is much larger than the initial functional organization.

7. The matrix organization permits giving attention to both "old" and "new" products as well as readily changing priorities. The matrix makes it possible to use quite different kinds of talent and permits a high degree of flexibility in using talent within a function.

8. The product- or project-type positions are excellent ways of providing generalist experience without big risk.

9. In a matrix organization there is often a tug-of-war for resources among product or project managers. This can help the top manager make optimum allocations.

10. The product/function matrix is an excellent "transition" stage in the evolution from a functional to a divisionalized organization.

11. The matrix organization is an excellent alternative when it is impossible to subdivide one or more major functions. For example, chemical and petrochemical manufacturers find that process technology does not lend to subdividing into neat profit centers. In some situations it is impossible to subdivide the field selling effort, yet the top manager doesn't want to accept the negative behavioral characteristics of a functional organization. The matrix organization enables him, in large part, to avoid these characteristics.

8

An Additional Case of Structure Planning

Background Data

This manufacturing organization is in the eastern United States. It is a very successful company, with a return on investment of 25 percent and a return on sales of 12 percent. The company has 60 percent of its market; however, the market growth for the basic business is expected to slow down over the next decade.

Most of the company's business is done in the United States, with some exporting. A considerable foreign market exists.

The products involve high technology. They require both competent and timely technical service for customers in widely dispersed geographic areas. There is considerable commonality of technology in the three basic product lines. There is also a strong likelihood that a customer will make use of two of the three lines. There is a great advantage to maintaining a common or pooled selling effort as long as possible.

The results from the previously suggested four steps for analyzing a current structure will now be presented.

Present Organization Structure

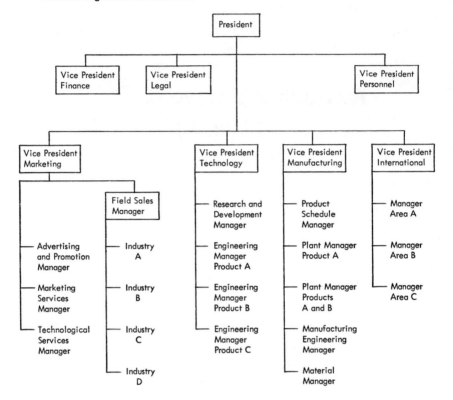

Step 1. Objectives of the Company

The following objectives were established, looking ten years ahead:

1. Double sales in the United States (from approximately $200 million to $400 million).

    Triple offshore sales (from $20 million to $60 million).

2. Maintain the historical rate of profit (25 percent return on investment, 12 percent return on sales).

3. Move into new but related business lines in a substantial way ($100 million in ten years).

4. Maintain market position in basic product lines.

5. Provide timely and effective technical service.

6. Remain nonunion.
7. Maintain technological leadership in the industry.
8. Secure, develop, and retain needed executives, managers, and critical technical personnel.

Step 2. Obstacles of the Company

The following obstacles were established. They are not listed in order of importance. Each is considered to be important.

1. The current functional organization has difficulty in being profit oriented or concerned.
2. The engineering function dominates trade-off decisions at the expense of overall results.
3. There is difficulty in getting needed management data and information for management control.
4. The company is not really committed to offshore effort.
5. There is a limited and inconsistent effort to add new product lines.
6. Competition is becoming increasingly severe.
7. Cost pressures, particularly on manufacturing, are steadily increasing.
8. There is considerable turnover in personnel, personnel development efforts are inadequate, and some personnel policies are obsolete.
9. There is inadequate teamwork across functional groups.
10. There has been a slippage on delivery dates, due in large part to an increase in quality problems.
11. Business planning has been ineffective to date.

Step 3. Organizational Criteria versus Present Structure

Criteria	*Status of Present Structure*
1. Positions needed to facilitate specialization	
a. By product line: A, B, and new product. (Needed for trade-off decisions and control of profits. This is a critical need.)	No positions concerned about product in Marketing, some product groups in Engineering and Manufacturing
b. By major function: Technology, Manufacturing, Marketing. (Needed to achieve required operating results.)	Achieved for major functions
c. By customer for field selling and service. (Unique technology requirements of major customer types make this a real leverage opportunity over competition.)	Achieved within field selling and service component
d. By geographic areas —offshore	Achieved by International component

Criteria	*Status of Present Structure*
e. By new product lines. (Needed to facilitate trade-off decisions, particularly across Technology and Marketing.)	Not achieved by present structure. Some positions at lower level than present chart pertain to products
2. Positions needed to facilitate control	
a. Profitability of major product lines. (This is a critical need to maintain profit rates. Must operate across major functions.)	Done now by President
b. International effort	Vice President International
c. Getting new business.	No position exists on present chart
d. Product line control across industries within Marketing	Done now only by Vice President Marketing
e. Quality control	Positions exist below plant manager level
f. Personnel	Vice President Personnel
3. Positions needed to facilitate coordination	
a. Across major functions	Done now only by President

Criteria	*Status of Present Structure*
b. Across product lines	No position
c. Across domestic and offshore efforts	President plus Vice President International
d. Moving a new product line into major functions	No position
4. Positions needed to insure that management attention is given to objectives or obstacles	
a. Acquiring, developing, and retaining personnel	No second level position. Some contribution by Vice President Personnel
b. Business planning	No position
c. Teamwork	Teamwork not part Vice President Personnel position as designed
d. Patents	One patent attorney under Vice President Legal
5. Positions needed to facilitate development, motivation, and retention of key personnel	
a. Generalist positions other than that of President needed	No such positions exist
b. Position needed to deal with personnel problems, particu-	Only partially achieved now

Criteria	*Status of Present Structure*
larly in International	
c. Position needed to provide experience in directing across all subfunctions in Marketing	No such position exists
6. Achieving organization structure at minimum cost	
a. Any unnecessary positions?	Not at the top three levels
b. Any unnecessary levels of management?	Not at the top three levels
c. Any narrow spans?	The three Staff Vice President positions (not shown on chart) have narrow spans
d. Any misplaced positions?	Research and Development Manager's position may be a level low

Step 4. Organizational Alternatives

Two quite different alternative organizations were considered. One was to set up product divisions; the other was to use a product/functional matrix. A diagram of each structure will be presented, followed by an analysis against the benefits used in Step 3.

ALTERNATIVE A

Product/Functional Matrix

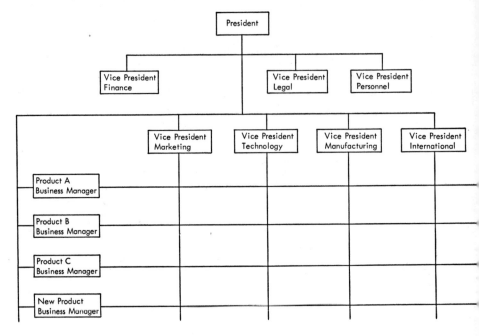

ALTERNATIVE B

Product Divisions

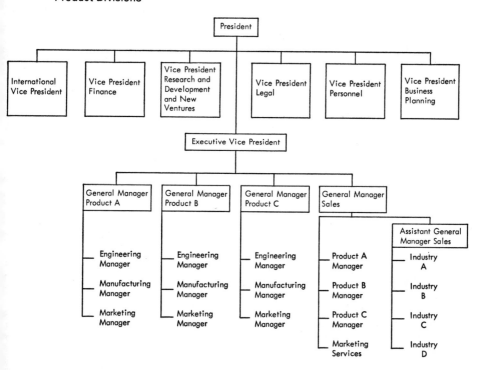

	Alternative A (product/functional matrix)	Alternative B (product divisions)
1. Positions needed to facilitate specialization		
a. By product line: A, B, and new product. (Needed for trade-off decisions and control of profits. This is a critical need.)	Four positions reporting to President	Three General Managers. (They must rely on pooled sales.)
b. By major function: Technology, Manufacturing, Marketing. (Needed to achieve required operating results.)	Four major functions report to President	Sales remains company-wide. Other functions subdivided, drop down a level (a significant change)
c. By customer for field selling and service. (Unique technology requirements of major customer types make this a real leverage opportunity over competition.)	Four positions in field selling	Four positions in field selling
d. By geographic areas—offshore	Achieved for offshore with Product Manager overlay	Vice President International plus General Managers with offshore responsibility by product
e. By new product lines. (Needed to facilitate trade-off decisions across Technology and Marketing.)	A Business Manager for new products	A Vice President on new ventures, combined with Research and Development

2. Positions needed to facilitate control		
a. Profitability of major product lines	Three Business Managers reporting to President	Three Product General Managers reporting to an Executive Vice-President (Product General Managers must depend on pooled selling effort.)
b. International effort	A Vice President International (same as on current chart).	A Vice President International (same as on current chart)
c. Getting new business	New Product Business Manager	A New Ventures Manager reporting directly to President
d. Product line control across industries within Marketing	Three Product Managers in Marketing (not shown on chart)	Three Product Managers in Marketing
e. Quality control	Positions exist below Manufacturing Manager level	Positions exist below Manufacturing Manager level
f. Personnel	Vice President Personnel	Vice President Personnel
3. Positions needed to facilitate co-ordination		
a. Across major functions	Three Product Business Managers plus New Product Business Manager	Three Product General Managers.
b. Across product lines	President across Product Business Managers	Executive Vice President position across Product General Managers
c. Across domestic and offshore efforts	President and Vice President International along with Product Business Managers	President and Vice President International along with three Product Business Managers.
d. Moving a new product line into major functions	New Product Business Manager	New Ventures Manager

	Alternative A (product/functional matrix)	Alternative B (product divisions)
4. Positions needed to insure that management attention is given to objectives or obstacles		
a. Acquiring, developing, and retaining personnel	Management Development Manager (not shown on chart)	Management Development Manager (not shown on chart)
b. Business planning	Product Business Managers	Vice President Business Planning and Product General Managers
c. Teamwork	Revision of Vice President Personnel position	Revision of Vice President Personnel position
d. Patents	Same as on current chart—one position	Same as on current chart—one position
5. Positions needed to facilitate development, motivation, and retention of key personnel		
a. Generalist positions needed other than that of President	Four new generalist positions	Three new generalist positions
b. Positions needed to deal with personnel problems, particularly in International	No change from current chart	No change from current chart
c. Position needed to provide experience in directing across all subfunctions in Marketing	Product Business Managers get some experience with entire marketing process	Product Managers get some experience with entire marketing process

6. Achieving organization structure at minimum cost

a. Any unnecessary positions?	Not at top three levels	Not at top three levels
b. Any unnecessary levels of management?	Four new Product General Manager positions created deemed necessary	Three new General Manager positions plus Executive Vice President position deemed necessary
c. Any narrow spans?	No change, except to add four positions to span of President	President's position subdivided
d. Any misplaced positions?	No change from present chart	No change from present chart

part three
Power

Power is the ability to influence, to have an impact upon decisions and actions. An individual has power when he can make something happen.

Authority is one aspect of power. If granted formally, authority may give an individual the right to decide or act. It may also be considered a restriction.

Comments about Power

George A. Smith, Jr.,[1] studied geographically decentralized companies in the mid-50s. He was one of the first writers on organization planning to stress the importance of power. He found that in their organization planning, few companies thought through the problem of how decisions ought to be made.

Smith identified certain significant problems that divisionalized companies find most stubborn and most widespread.* Among the problems were:

---

* See bibliography for details on each reference.

1. Friction between central and local officers.
2. Jockeying for power (headquarters officers versus local officers).
3. Resistance to changed status relationships.
4. The tendency of people at each level to overstep prescribed bounds.

Douglas McGregor[2] was a behavioral scientist who was concerned about power. In his last book, prepared shortly before his untimely death, he devoted a chapter to managerial power. McGregor drew the following implications from behavioral science knowledge:

1. Management should become selective in its exercise of power.
2. Quite different forms of power are available.
3. Managers need to recognize the limitations of traditional forms of power.
4. Legitimate authority is one form of power. However, it is neither a God-given nor a logical right. The "consent of the governed" is more than a pious phrase.
5. The exercise of legitimate authority can minimize behavior opposed to organizational goals. It does not maximize enthusiastic support of these goals.
6. The direct control of extrinsic rewards and punishments is a second form of power.
7. Managers should not place primary reliance on extrinsic rewards as a means of obtaining the desired contributions to organizational goals.
8. A third form of power rests on identification. Individuals genuinely identify themselves with a group, a leader, or a cause. It is in connection with identification that leadership becomes a source of power.
9. The paradox is that where there is high identification, with its concomitant commitment to goals, the exercise

of authority and other external forms of power becomes both more effective and less necessary.

10. Identification is a potent source of power whose value is often underestimated.

11. Social influence—the exercise of power—is thus a far more difficult and complex process than is typically understood by such labels as hard, soft, or firm—but fair—strategies of management.

Peter Drucker[3] suggests that there is need for a decision-focused organizational design principle. He regards decisions as being as much a dimension of management as work and task, results and performance, and relations. As he looked around the landscape Drucker was unable to discern such a principle. It seems to me that the stress on power in this book, and the use of decisions as a means of managing power, do provide, at least in a preliminary manner, the principle Drucker is looking for.

Abraham Zaleznick[4] argues that competition for power is found in all political structures and that business organizations, whatever else they may be, are certainly political structures. Zaleznick stresses the following concepts:

1. People compete for power. One individual's gain is likely to be another's loss.

2. An individual's sense of possessing power and his sense of self-esteem develop in parallel.

3. Top executives often act ineffectively in resolving power issues because of their fear of rivalry. That fear often leads to paranoid thinking. This causes powerful people to develop massive blind spots which limit vision. Paranoid thinking goes beyond suspiciousness, distrust, and jealousy. It may take the form of grandiose ideas and overestimation of one's power and control.

4. Power conflicts often lead to the establishment of ritualis-

tic procedures and other ceremonials which create the illusion of solving problems, but serve only to discharge valuable energies ineffectively.

5. There is an ongoing process of negotiation and compromise among executives who hold semiautonomous power bases (baronies).

6. The emotional stability or maturity of an executive greatly influences the effectiveness with which power problems are resolved.

Norman Martin and John Howard Sims[5] proposed that executives make effective use of power tactics. A brief summary of their tactics follows.

> In such a light, we see why the successful functioning and advancement of the executive is dependent, not only on those aspects of an enterprise which are physical and logical, but on morale, teamwork, authority, and obedience—in a word, on the vast intricacy of human relationships which make up the political universe of the executive.
>
> The real question then becomes: How can power be used most effectively? What are some of the political stratagems which the administrator must employ if he is to carry out his responsibilities and further his career?

Martin and Sims present some findings of the first stage of a fairly extensive investigation of just how the executive functions in his political power environment. They searched the biographies of well-known historic leaders, from Alexander the Great to Franklin Delano Roosevelt; they explored the lives of successful industrialists, such as John D. Rockefeller and Henry Ford; and they interviewed a number of contemporary executives. The tactics they suggest follow:

1. Taking Counsel. The able executive is cautious about how he seeks and receives advice. He takes counsel only when he himself desires it. His decisions must be made in terms of his own grasp of the situation, taking into account the views of others only when he thinks this necessary. To act otherwise is to be subject, not to advice, but to pressure; to act otherwise too often produces vacillation and inconsistency.

2. Alliances. In many respects, the executive system in a firm is composed of complexes of sponsor-protégé relationships. A wise executive will make it a point to establish such associations with those above and below him. In the struggles for power and influence that go on in many organizations, every executive needs a devoted following and close alliances with other executives both on his own level and above it if he is to protect and to enhance his status and sphere of influence.

3. Maneuverability. The wise executive maintains his flexibility, and he never completely commits himself to any one position or program. He should preserve maneuverability in career planning as well. He ought never to get into a situation that does not have plenty of escape hatches. He must be careful, for instance, that his career is not directly dependent on the superior position of a sponsor.

4. Communication. During recent years emphasis has been placed on the necessity for well-dredged channels of communication which run upward, downward, and sideways. It is possible, however, that executives have been oversold on maximizing the flow of information. It simply is not good strategy to communicate everything one knows. Rather, it may often be advantageous to withhold information, or to time its release. This is especially true with reference to plans for the future—plans which may or may not materialize. It is also valid in the case of information that may create schism or conflict within the organization.

5. Compromising. The executive should accept compromise with tongue in cheek. While appearing to alter his views, he should continue to press forward toward a clear-cut set of goals.

6. Negative Timing. The executive is often urged to take action with which he is not in agreement. In such situations, he may find it wise to use what might be called the technique of "negative timing." He initiates action, but retards the expediting process.

7. Self-Dramatization. Executives would do well to re-examine this instinctive behavior, for many of them are overlooking an important political stratagem. The skill of an actor—whose communication is "artistic" as opposed to "natural"—represents a potential asset to an administrator. Dramatic art is a process by which selections from reality are chosen and arranged for the particular purposes of arousing the emotions, of convincing, of persuading, of altering behavior in a planned direction.

8. Confidence. Related to, but not identical with, self-dramatization is the outward appearance of confidence. Once an executive has made a decision, he must look and act decided.

9. Always the Boss. In practice an atmosphere of social friendship interferes with the efficiency of an operation and acts to limit the power of the executive. Personal feelings should not be a basis for action—either positive or negative. No matter how cordial he may be, the executive must sustain a line of privacy which cannot be transgressed; in the final analysis he must always be the boss. At the same time, he must develop some rationale of executive behavior which can encompass the idealism of democracy and the practicality of politics—and yet be justified in terms of ultimate values.

One way to try to fit human relations theory and political tactics together is to state that the means or ways of exercising power are neutral. In and of themselves, they have no moral value. They take on moral qualities only in connection with the ends for which they are used. Power can be used for good or ill, according to this view, and we should have the courage and the knowledge needed to use it wisely.

The previously cited writers span a considerable span of time. They reflect the fact that power has long been a "puzzlement." Power has gradually become a legitimate concern. Slowly, some tentative theories about the nature of power and how it might be "used" or "handled" have been propounded. The presence of power problems as a daily reality in all organizations suggests that managers must endeavor to grapple with such problems more effectively. Let us consider some typical power problems.

Typical Power Problems

The reader can share in the process of identifying typical power problems by thinking of other illustrations that might be added to the ones we will now consider.

Dominance by One Group. At any given level of an organization there are several groups. As has been noted in previous chapters, the general type of group reporting to the top manager is likely to be characterized by certain rather predictable behavior patterns. In addition, one group will often dominate other groups. It is quite common to refer to an organization as Marketing dominated, or Engineering dominated, or Finance dominated. If the dominant group is the component most critical to the success of an enterprise, dominance is likely to be appropriate and acceptable. However, if dominance by a group is based on other factors, this dominance isn't likely to be considered as legitimate by the nondominant groups. In these circumstances there is a potential for conflict.

Power Grabs. Power grabs aren't restricted to politicians. In many organizations, an individual will endeavor to move into a power vacuum, to grab power for himself. Such a drive for power reflects the individual's strong personal needs. The threat of power grabs by subordinates or peers often presents a challenge to the executive.

Intergroup Conflicts. The existence of intergroup conflict is frequently seen in such groups as:

—manufacturing and engineering.
—marketing and manufacturing.
—personnel and finance.

Up to a point, conflict serves a useful purpose. It permits specialized groups to advance their own views. Carried beyond that point, conflict becomes fruitless friction, often inhibiting the achievement of organizational results.

Decentralization Issues. There are numerous ways to decentralize. One is to shift from a large functional organization to product groups, usually called divisions. At the same time, a corporate staff group is established. The fundamental issue in divisionalizing is how much autonomy the top group is going to grant the lower level. Some organizations pride themselves on tight central control, others on granting real autonomy. In many organizations the power issues aren't dealt with deliberately. They get resolved on a case-by-case basis. Considerable ambiguity exists. Often there is an ebb and flow of power. During periods of adversity, power flows to the central group. During periods of success, power flows to the operating groups. Interestingly, some large organizations would lead you to believe that they are highly decentralized when they really grant heads of operating divisions few opportunities to make any significant decision on their own.

Delegation. Delegation can well be viewed as a problem of vertical power. How much power are successive levels of management expected to exercise? Often subordinates let decisions float up, to be made at a higher level. Often superiors, without realizing it, begin to operate at a lower level than the level at which they are being paid to operate.

Line- and Staff-Type Authority. Once a director of finance in a large company threatened to resign if the controllers in the operating divisions were shown as reporting to him by a dotted line on the organization chart rather than by a solid line. The nature of the lines, presumably, reflected something about power. The effort to differentiate between line- and staff-type authority, often by means of solid and dotted lines, is a crude way of coping with power issues.

Merger Power Issues. During the "honeymoon" period of a merger there is a strong likelihood that the two partners will not confront real power issues. To do so may jeopardize the merger. One large conglomerate with a long history of mergers has rarely been able to retain the original top managers of an acquired company. Unresolved power issues led them to leave, usually within the first year. The change from being one's own boss, often for many years, to reporting to a "professional manager," who is usually much younger, presents great difficulty for the acquired executive. A few organizations do deal with the power issues of mergers deliberately and effectively.

Importance of Power

Power has an important impact on the way individuals in an organization behave because of the relationship of power to:

1. Purpose.
2. Resources.
3. Ego needs.

We will examine each of these relationships in turn.

The definition of purpose, the decision on direction of the enterprise, is of great concern to the top executive and to each of his subordinates. Let's consider several illustrations.

1. The president of a large insurance company decided to expand into new businesses. His board didn't share his enthusiasms. He was asked to leave.

2. Three scientists formed their own technology-based organization. The one who became president was so enthusiastic about his speciality that soon all the firm's capital was being monopolized by his projects. This led to a disrupting of the relationship of the three men.

3. A large computer organization was considering a move into a new business arena. One group favored the move. Another didn't. Once the decision was made, the losing group quickly realized that they should go on to greener pastures.

It is impossible for an executive, no matter what his level, to change the direction of his particular enterprise or portion of an enterprise without confronting serious power problems. Recognizing this has led some executives to be quite ambiguous in defining the purpose and direction of their enterprises.

The relation of resources to power is quite direct. Every organization is resource limited. The resources may be money, talent, products, facilities, equipment, raw materials, customers, or time. Subgroups in an organization are in direct conflict for scarce resources. If one subgroup has a power advantage, it may capture an unfair share of the organization's scarce resources. The leader of a subgroup represents both himself and his group. His success as a leader is dramatically revealed by how effectively he competes for resources in short supply.

The ego needs of managers are also directly related to power. Some managers have a driving ambition to exert power; others prefer not to exert power; still others prefer not to be in a situation where somebody exerts power over them. Some managers want to make the critical decisions; other managers prefer to buck all such decisions to a higher level.

Fortune magazine recently reported upon the decision of a rising young executive to leave a handsome salary in a large enterprise. One reason given for the change was the frustration he experienced when he found out how power was really exercised at the very top of the enterprise. It was suggested that the group or committee nature of the process turned him off. The importance of power is due, therefore, to the critical relationship between power and purpose, resources and ego needs. Managers cannot avoid power problems. However, they can choose whether to anticipate such problems deliberately or to cope with them as they arise. Managers who take the latter course will often find themselves dealing with symptoms. We will argue that executives can and should deal with power issues and power problems in a much more deliberate and effective manner than is often the case.

We are not urging the avoidance of conflict. Conflict is a desirable benefit of various structural alternatives. But conflict must be managed. Purposeful conflict is the desired end; fruitless friction should be kept at a minimum.

In the remaining chapters of Part Three, attention will be given to the subjects "analyzing power problems" and "managing power."

9

Analyzing Power Problems

The Decision to Analyze

In this chapter we will concern ourselves with a manager who decides to analyze power problems within his own organization. He can analyze and deal with such power problems directly. However, if a power problem involves the manager's group and another group, the decision to analyze it requires the cooperation of the "opponents." In some instances, a power problem may involve a manager and his superior. Here, the problem might be analyzed by the subordinate, but its resolution would require the collaboration of the superior.

Numerous clues suggest the existence of a power problem. Conflict between two individuals or groups which goes beyond the airing of constructive differences is certainly one such clue. Character assassination efforts, which are often reciprocated, are another clue. Evidence that individuals are overstepping the bounds of their authority or that they aren't exercising their authority is also a definite clue to the existence of a power problem.

Often there is agreement that communication is not what it should be. In some of these instances, there is actually a lack of meaningful interaction or interchange. But more often than not, complaints about poor communication are symptomatic of power problems.

The decision to analyze power problems requires that a manager:

1. Recognize that a potential power problem exists.
2. Decide that the adverse effects warrant some action.
3. Be willing to risk heated confrontations and related phenomena.
4. Decide on a method of analysis.

A consideration of analytic methods is in order. I have found four to be quite helpful. Other methods are mentioned in the literature. A new technology called Organization Development[6] features methods of analyzing and resolving power conflicts. It is most important for managers to recognize that they can move from a concern about conflict and other power problems to processes of analysis and resolution.

Method 1. Critical Decision Analysis

Let us assume that the general manager of a manufacturing division has a manufacturing group and an engineering group who appear to have power problems. Conflicts between the two groups occur frequently, and the general manager finds problems being bucked up to him which should be resolved at a lower level.

The general manager decides to use the Critical Decision Analysis method. It is helpful to have a neutral staff individual actually initiate the analysis. The analysis involves the following steps.

Step 1. A number of decisions of concern to both groups are identified. The following decisions are likely to be considered critical by engineering-manufacturing groups.

1. When can an engineering change be introduced by engineering?
2. When can an engineering change be deferred or vetoed by manufacturing?
3. Who has the right to say when a part or a product meets specifications?
4. How much lead time is required to introduce a major engineering change? What is a major engineering change?
5. What changes can manufacturing make to facilitate manufacturability?
6. When a default becomes critical to consumer acceptance, how can we most quickly and accurately determine whether engineering or manufacturing or both are responsible?

Step 2. The individual groups define their respective roles for each decision. The engineering group is then asked to define the role they feel is most appropriate for engineering with regard to each of the above decisions. This needs to be done quite thoroughly. The engineering group might say: "Engineering has the sole right to decide what engineering changes are needed and when they should be introduced. In making such decisions, engineering will give consideration to our competitive position, safety requirements, and the cost of the changes."

The manufacturing group is also asked to define the role they should play with regard to each decision. The manufacturing group might conclude, for example, that they should determine the cost of any engineering changes and that they should have the right to appeal any engineering change being made if the cost of the change exceeds a certain amount.

Step 3. Each group defines the other group's role for each decision. The reverse side of the coin calls for the engineering group to define the role manufacturing should play regarding each decision. An engineering group might well say: "Manufacturing should analyze how soon a change can be made and how much it will cost. Within reason, manufacturing can schedule the timing of the change."

The term *within reason* is, of course, vague. This vagueness will probably lead to heated discussions in subsequent steps.

Similarly, the manufacturing group defines the role of engineering. They might put it this way: "Engineering should decide what engineering changes are desirable. They should then talk with manufacturing about the impact of the changes. They have the right to say what should be changed. They don't have the right to say exactly when the changes will be made."

Step 4. A confrontation session between the two groups is held. The neutral staff man sets up a confrontation session with the two groups. Flip charts of the four positions are prepared and presented. These conference strategies make for fruitful confrontation sessions:

1. Once the entire flip chart presentation of role definitions has been made, only clarification questions are permitted.

2. The issues selected for initial discussion should not be too critical. They should be issues on which the differences aren't too great and on which a resolution is likely to be

achieved. In any case, the real issues, which concern how power is going to be utilized by each group, are placed on top of the table.

3. It should be recognized that critical differences may take a long time to work out. Stress is placed upon the need to have decisions made in the best interest of the larger organization. The process, in effect, says, "Let functional groups be egocentric; let them do their best to be successful. However, when they prevent other groups from being successful, then the issue needs to be joined and resolved, not on a win-lose basis, but on a 'larger good' basis."

The results of the confrontation session can be converted into policy statements, standard operating procedures, and other reference documents. It is quite possible that a repeat session will be necessary after a year or so.

The first three steps can be completed by a staff man interviewing individuals or it can be done by group interviews. The entire process can be part of an all-day conference in which engineering and manufacturing work as subgroups on the initial steps.

The above illustration involved a two-group power problem. However, the process works equally well with a larger number of groups. The main difference is that it takes much longer to complete each step when three or more groups are involved.

Method 2.   Decision Chain Analysis

Some work flows cut across several groups. Among such work flows are:

1.   The new product sequence from concept to market introduction.

2. The design, construction, and start-up of a plant.
3. The recruitment, selection, and orientation of new employees.
4. Order entry to final shipping and billing.

As often as not, such work flows have evolved over a period of time, during which they have usually become quite complex. The computer has often forced a thorough analysis and standardization. In many instances, there is no comprehensive description of the work flow and the respective contributions to be made by each group.

Let's consider an abbreviated example of a decision chain analysis. In actual practice more steps would be involved, more groups would be involved, and the definition of each contribution would be more detailed.

The following steps are involved in a decision chain analysis:

1. All groups that contribute to the work flow are identified.
2. Major segments of the work flow are identified.
3. Each group defines the contribution it feels it should make in each major segment. Particular attention is given to the decisions each group feels it makes.
4. The results of steps 1 through 3 are reduced to a written diagram.
5. The diagram will reveal differences involving two or more groups. These differences need to be worked out in discussion sessions. The sessions are similar to the confrontation step of the Critical Decision Analysis.
6. The final diagram of the decision chain is reduced to writing. It becomes a reference document which permits periodic reviews and revisions to be made readily.

An Example of a Decision Chain Analysis for an Equipment Machinery Manufacturer

Decisions	General Manager	Engineering Director	Marketing Director	Manufacturing Director
1. Need for a major new feature	Suggests need for a new feature as a basic strategy. Makes decision to proceed	Suggests opportunity based on a breakthrough	Suggests need based on customer contacts	Suggests need from a cost-saving standpoint
2. Design of new feature	Final decision (shared with Engineering Director)	Schedules project effort. Prepares preliminary design. Final decision (shared with General Manager)	Advises on design from customer point of view	Advises on feasibility of manufacturing, cost, and purchasing considerations
3. Timing introduction of new feature	Final decision		Suggests desired marketing schedule	Suggests desired manufacturing schedule
4. Price revision	Final decision		Recommends amount and timing	
5. Introduction of new feature to customer		Makes decision on any design modifications which may be made	Advertising prepares introductory program. Field sales synchronizes with ad schedule	
6. Evaluation			Reports on pros and cons of new feature at appropriate intervals	

Method 3.   Authority Study

This method has to do with a vertical power problem. It is sometimes referred to as the delegation challenge. Managers often work a level lower than they are being paid. Subordinates often develop an uncanny ability to delegate upward. Admonitions to delegate more or to take on more responsibility seldom prove fruitful. The authority study provides a description of how vertical power is currently being exercised. This description serves as a springboard for changing conditions which are deemed to be less than optimum.

Let's consider the steps required in conducting an authority study for a group of middle-level supervisors.

Step 1. Fifteen or 20 important decisions are selected. These are decisions which may be made either by a supervisor or by the supervisor's manager. The decisions selected should include ones which are often made improperly.

Step 2. A worksheet is completed by each supervisor. For each decision the supervisor indicates whether he:

1.   Makes the decision or takes action on his own.
2.   Makes the decision, but informs his superior.
3.   Talks with someone else (boss or other) before deciding, *but decides himself.*
4.   Makes a recommendation, but leaves the decision to someone else.
5.   Takes no action.

Step 3. A worksheet is completed by the supervisors' manager. The manager may set a uniform pattern for all supervisors. If so, this constitutes a "standard." It is also possible that a manager's responses will be slightly different for each supervisor.

AUTHORITY STUDY (SUPERVISOR)

	a. I make the decision or take action on my own without talking to anyone.	b. I make the decision or take action and then inform my superior.	c. I discuss the situation with someone else before making the decision.	d. I recommend what should be done, but someone else makes the decision.	e. I take no action.

Listed below are various circumstances which may require a supervisor to make a decision or take action.

Select from the five responses the one which most closely applies to the way you would deal with each circumstance.

Assume that the statements apply to personnel under your supervision.

Circumstance	a	b	c	d	e
1. Paid overtime becomes necessary.					
2. An employee requests personal time off.					
3. A choice among several candidates for employment must be made.					
4. A choice among several candidates for promotion must be made.					
5. The time to consider a salary change for a subordinate has arrived.					
6. The behavior of one of your employees requires a verbal reprimand.					
7. An employee's poor performance seems to warrant termination of employment.					
8. The time for an annual performance appraisal of a subordinate has arrived.					
9. It is necessary to reassign personnel to new duties.					
10. A new position appears to be needed.					
11. A requested major equipment repair must be scheduled.					
12. Equipment which is deemed unsafe must be shut down.					
13. Changed priorities on scheduled work are required in order to maintain a steady work flow.					
14. It is necessary to discuss an employee's personal problem with the employee.					
15. It is time to revise priorities on work to be done in your group.					

Completed by: _____ Date _____

AUTHORITY STUDY (MANAGER)

Listed below are various circumstances which may require a supervisor who reports to you to make a decision or take action.

Select from the five responses the one which most closely applies to the way you would want your supervisors to deal with each circumstance.

a. He makes the decision or takes action on his own without talking to anyone.

b. He makes the decision or takes action and then informs his superior.

c. He discusses the situation with someone else before making the decision.

d. He recommends what should be done, but someone else makes the decision.

e. He takes no action.

	a	b	c	d	e
1. Paid overtime becomes necessary.					
2. An employee requests personal time off.					
3. A choice among several candidates for employment must be made.					
4. A choice among several candidates for promotion must be made.					
5. The time to consider a salary change for a subordinate has arrived.					
6. The behavior of one of your employees requires a verbal reprimand.					
7. An employee's poor performance seems to warrant termination of employment.					
8. The time for an annual performance appraisal of a subordinate has arrived.					
9. It is necessary to reassign personnel to new duties.					
10. A new position appears to be needed.					
11. A requested major equipment repair must be scheduled.					
12. Equipment which is deemed unsafe must be shut down.					
13. Changed priorities on scheduled work are required in order to maintain a steady work flow.					
14. It is necessary to discuss an employee's personal problem with the employee.					
15. It is time to revise priorities on work to be done in your group.					

Completed by:_____ Date_____

Step 4. Each supervisor's replies are compared with the manager's standard. Variances are identified. The more critical variances become the first order of discussion.

Step 5. Resolution of differences. The resolutions can be accomplished on a one-to-one basis or in a group session. The outcome should be a common understanding between the manager and each supervisor on how the latter is to handle each decision.

It will be helpful to review the Authority Study Worksheets used in the above study.

The authority study illustrated was for a supervisor. The process has also been used to examine the respective responsibilities of a president and a group vice president. It has proven helpful at all levels of a management hierarchy.

Method 4.   Staff-Line Analysis

Most organizations have several groups who are thought of as "line." These groups share the basic work, such as designing, making, and selling. Then there are "staff" groups who do support work. Staff groups often present interesting power problems. The top manager may decide to use them as control groups. He may give them veto power over certain decisions. Staff executives often shift from offering advice to giving orders. In some instances line managers object to having staff persons make decisions. In other instances they are quite willing to let staff persons take the responsibility for decisions. For reasons such as the above, ambiguity prevails in the relationship between line and staff groups.

The Staff-Line Analysis method is designed to eliminate this ambiguity. Let us assume that we are talking about a large manufacturing plant in which several superintendents and a personnel director report to the plant manager. The Staff-Line Analysis would involve the following steps:

Step 1. A list of 15 to 20 personnel function contributions is formulated. This might include contributions now being made, contributions that could be made, and contributions that the superintendents would prefer not be made.

Step 2. The superintendents are asked to indicate the extent to which they are currently getting a given contribution. They are also asked to indicate whether they would like to see more or less effort given to that contribution.

Step 3. The personnel group are asked to establish their position for each contribution.

Step 4. A confrontation session is held to resolve the differences between the two views.

The example of contributions used in a study of a personnel group illustrates how the steps can be accomplished.

Confrontation Processes

In each of the above methods, two groups are asked to provide certain data in advance. The data are likely to reveal divergent views. One or more confrontation sessions are held to resolve the divergent views. Certain processes have proven useful in making such sessions productive:

1. The use of a neutral leader.
2. Spending initial time in a clarification of the respective positions. This encourages the groups to view the positions of their opponents more objectively.
3. Avoiding a win-lose outcome. An effort should be made to come up with an integrating solution in which both sides are "successful."

Personnel Relations Survey

Please indicate current frequency by circling one answer to the left of each statement.	Please indicate your future ex-pectations by circling one answer to the right of each statement.

Quite Frequently
Frequently
Occasionally
Rarely
Never

Do more of this
Do about the same as now
Do less of this
Does not apply

QF F O R N   1. I alert managers to relations problems in the organization.   M S L D

QF F O R N   2. I advise managers when I think some of their management practices are having an adverse impact on operating results and/or morale.   M S L D

QF F O R N   3. I review critical relations decisions or actions to be taken by operating managers to insure that they are appropriate (has to do with grievances, arbitrations, salary changes, etc.).   M S L D

QF F O R N   4. I design relations policies, procedures, and programs.   M S L D

QF F O R N   5. I install relations procedures and programs.   M S L D

QF F O R N   6. I follow up on relations policies, procedures, and programs to see that they are working.   M S L D

QF F O R N   7. I conduct studies to help managers improve on their way of managing.   M S L D

QF F O R N   8. I conduct studies of important relations problems and recommend action.   M S L D

Personnel Relations Survey (*Continued*)

		Please indicate current frequency by circling one answer to the left of each statement.	Please indicate your future expectations by circling one answer to the right of each statement.	

Quite Frequently / Frequently / Occasionally / Rarely / Never			Do more of this / Do about the same as now / Do less of this / Does not apply

QF F O R N	9. I act as a personal confidant to key managers on individual and organizational problems.	M S L D
QF F O R N	10. I act as a counselor to nonsupervisory employees.	M S L D
QF F O R N	11. I act as a counselor to other managers on personal and organizational problems.	M S L D
QF F O R N	12. I analyze and act to insure that there is an adequate supply of skills and talents coming into the organization.	M S L D
QF F O R N	13. I am actively involved in maximum utilization of skills and abilities (managerial and nonsupervisory) to accomplish the objectives of the organization.	M S L D
QF F O R N	14. I am actively involved in the process of evaluating managerial skills and abilities.	M S L D
QF F O R N	15. I contribute analysis and advice on key staffing decisions.	M S L D
QF F O R N	16. I contribute to determination and design of the organization structure.	M S L D
QF F O R N	17. I participate in major discussions pertaining to the organization's objectives and goals and to their achievement.	M S L D

The above four methods of analysis are representative of the means by which a manager can shift from anxiety about power problems to a process of grappling with them. It is unlikely that power problems will be solved. However, their more adverse consequences can be minimized by the skillful use of analytic methods.

10

Managing Power

It may seem strange for me to suggest that power can and should be managed. But that is exactly what I would like to do. What does the term *managing power* mean? It means that a manager will be deliberate about deciding how power will be allocated and how it will be exercised. It also means that he will be deliberate about analyzing and modifying prevailing practices pertaining to power.

In this chapter we will look at the challenge of managing power from four angles:

1. Indirect methods of allocating power.
2. Formal methods of allocating power.
3. Historical organizational "principles" pertaining to power that can be ignored.
4. Some process suggestions for allocating power.

Indirect Methods of Allocating Power

The indirect methods of allocating power aren't often thought of as being susceptible to deliberate action. However,

124

the indirect methods often outweigh the formal efforts. Therefore, it behooves a manager to be aware of the informal
methods and to use them deliberately.

Involvement in Decision Making. No matter what the style
of decision making, there is a distinct advantage to being in
the group in which critical decisions are made. An autocrat
may make a decision with little imput from subordinates.
However, being among those close to the autocrat when a decision is made does make it possible to at least attempt to
exert influence. In any case, being in that group gives one immediate knowledge of decisions and of the circumstances sur-
rounding them.

With a participative style of decision making, being part of
the decision-making group permits one to influence and be
influenced in decision making.

Easy Access. The opportunity to readily enter a superior's
office has interesting power implications. It enables one to
provide information and to insure that one's own position is
considered in all decisions. This is particularly helpful in
conflict situations.

Recreational Activities. Managers often have a favorite
sport, such as golfing or fishing. A subordinate who can become regularly involved in such recreational activity with a
superior, acquires a potential power advantage.

Office Location. It is interesting to note that some corpora-
tions force their top group executives to situate their offices
in the corporate headquarters location. It is easier to exert
power over an individual if he is nearby.

It is also interesting to note who has the office nearest to
that of the superior and who has the one farthest removed. In
some organizations the finance manager is always found in
the adjacent office.

While we would not necessarily consider periodic "musical chairs" changing of offices, it is still desirable to be deliberate about office locations.

Status Perquisites. Numerous perquisites provide status. Among them are: office decor, number and age of secretaries, reserved parking, company airplane priority, attendance at top management conferences, executive physical examination, and incentive compensation.

Usually an executive will treat all of his direct reports on a uniform basis. However, over a period of time small inconsistencies begin to occur. They take on significance from a power viewpoint. Somewhat subtly, a "pecking order" becomes established. Here again, the plea isn't necessarily for uniformity in the allocation of "pecks," but for recognizing their power implications and being deliberate in their distribution.

Titles. In some companies the title "manager, marketing" is lower in status than the title "marketing manager." The title "vice president" often carries weight with it. The power implications of titles become important when some subordinates have a title such as "vice president" and others on the same level don't. The importance attached to titles is revealed by a large utility. One of its unwritten laws is that only a vice president can write a letter to another vice president.

There are many reasons for being quite deliberate in the use of titles. One reason is that titles can be used as a calculated means of allocating power.

Traditional Dominance of One Group. Often the exercise of power is influenced by the fact that one function has historically dominated the business. In a newly formed technological company, the engineering function usually dominates. In a consumer product company, the marketing component usually dominates. The traditional dominance is sometimes appropriate. Often it isn't. When it isn't, optimum results become difficult to get unless that dominance is kept under control.

Formal Methods of Allocating Power

Let us consider the formal means by which a manager can allocate power within an organization.

The Right to Decide. The formal method most frequently used is the right to decide.

The right to decide may be stated as a limitation. For example:

-- New equipment may be purchased which does not cost more than $50,000.

-- New personnel can be hired as long as the approved manning schedule is not exceeded.

The right to decide may be stated in positive terms. For example:

-- Pricing decisions are to be made by the division general manager.

-- Salary increases can be approved for everyone under your supervision.

Often an authority table is prepared showing the right to decide on a series of decisions for a series of positions.

The Right to Act. This formal method is closely related to the right to decide. It implies a right to implement a decision once the decision has been made. For example:

-- You have the right to discharge any employee under your supervision for proper cause.

-- You can take a union grievance to arbitration.

The Right to Veto. This is an interesting allocation of power. The top manager may wish to avoid certain risks. So he grants a partial right to decide to a subordinate. At the same time, he grants the right to veto this decision to a second subordinate. The veto usually results from the authority of knowledge, such as legal knowledge or knowledge of the terms of a union contract. It may also result from an organization-wide view, such as an awareness of the impact on a customer of decisions made by several components.

The Right to Audit. The right to audit is a power which is most apparent in the financial audit. However, it may be applied to many other areas, such as product quality or the legality of decisions.

The Obligation to Review. A process may be established in which a manager is obligated to review with one or more individuals a decision or a possible action before it is carried out. The reviewers may or may not be granted the right to veto.

The Right to Influence. This may be thought of as a typical way of defining staff authority. We prefer to consider it as one other formal way of allocating power. It will often be used with so-called staff groups. However, it might also be used with one function in regard to another.

The Obligation of Joint Decision. A top manager might permit action to be taken only when agreement has been reached by two parties. For example, the top manager of an automotive company may permit a style decision to be implemented only when the central styling group and the operating group are in agreement.

The Opportunity to Protest. This isn't a very strong grant of power. Rather, it is a recourse to higher authority that an executive resorts to when he believes that some decision or action is being taken which is detrimental to his component.

Historical Organizational "Principles" Pertaining to Power that Can Be Ignored

As one wades through the literature on organization, one finds a considerable number of so-called principles that really deserve to be ignored. In some instances, they are simply incorrect. In other instances, they are not operational, that is, no means can be devised for putting them into effect. In still other instances, they are irrelevant or inconsequential.

Authority should be delegated equal to responsibility. Have you ever seen anybody trying to act on this hoary principle? How did he do it? The implication that delegation should occur is fine. The implication that power should be pushed downward in a hierarchical organization is valid. I sometimes tell managers that they would be hard pressed to justify their salaries if they limited themselves to objectives which were completely under their control. However, as Louis Allen[^] argues, this principle is a misconception. A person can never be given exactly as much authority as is required by the work he is assigned. Allen suggests that authority can only be delegated "commensurate" with responsibility. Operationally, one has a difficult time even deciding when delegation has become "commensurate."

The "line" decides, the "staff" advises. At one time this principle may well have reflected the way managers wanted things to be. But we have seen that in current practice the so-called staff position can have quite varying amounts of power. At one extreme, an individual in a staff position may be authorized, under some circumstances, to give orders to occupants of line positions. He may also have the right to veto line decisions. At the opposite extreme, the individual in a staff position may be required to confine himself to advice or persuasion. The more germane suggestion is that a manager be deliberate about how power is to be exercised in each and every position—line or staff. What should determine the manager's decision in each instance is the appropriateness of the powers exercised, not the function—line or staff—of those who exercise it.

Centralization is retaining decisions at relatively high organizational levels; decentralization is pushing decision making to lower organizational levels. I would argue that the terms *centralization* and *decentralization* are a crude way of talking about vertical power. To be operational, one has to be deliberate about identifying decisions and determining the most appropriate levels for making them. There is no particular harm in talk about the need for more centralization, or for more decentralization. Such talk just isn't very helpful when you decide to do something about changing the way decisions are made.

Some Process Suggestions for Allocating Power

1. *Allocate power to a position.* As we noted in the discussion of structure, a position is established to accomplish certain objectives or to overcome certain obstacles. In designing structure, we very deliberately avoided adapting structures to personalities. To those readers who wish to argue that personalities are a fact of life and must be taken into account, we would say, "Wait until Part V." When you get to staffing decisions, we will permit personalities to be taken into account. This may mean modifying your original decisions on structure, power, and job design. But at this stage we would repeat: Allocate power to a position. Keep to a minimum modifications due to personalities. Often this means an allocation of power to similar positions at a given level of management.

2. *Avoid giving one peer group power over another peer*

group. It is only fair play that every individual reporting to the same superior should have an equal opportunity to succeed. It is not only fair play but a necessity that each function be successful. Giving one peer group power over other peer groups should be avoided, if at all possible. For example, the finance director should not have the final say on the budgets of his peers, though he may be expected to advise and counsel his superior on those budgets. The industrial relations director should not have the power to dictate a peer's final grievance decision. The manufacturing manager may well be required to consult with the industrial relations staff. But that is quite different from permitting the industrial relations staff to make decisions for manufacturing.

Sometimes a top manager will decide that it is absolutely essential to give one peer power over other peers. In such a situation I would suggest that the power be allocated on a temporary basis and that the peer groups over whom that power is exercised should have timely recourse on all decisions with which they are in strong disagreement.

3. *Watch your measurement and reward system.* Often individuals on a given level have to work together to achieve optimum results. However, the measurement system used in such instances may report on each individual's *personal* success or lack thereof. The reward system based on such measurements often penalizes a team player. Rewards go to the individual who achieves *his* results, even though he may seriously handicap the groups with whom he should be working.

Many organizations get "oversexed" on measurements. Careers rise and fall on the basis of this quarter's financial results. In environments placing such great stress on measurements, there is likely to be considerable conflict over the way power is being allocated.

4. *Be extremely careful about telling an individual that he has profit responsibility.* In their enthusiasm for improving financial results, many organizations have rushed into "profit-centers." Such centers are seen as a way of getting a manager to react as he would if he were running his own business. Let's ignore the possibility that we shouldn't get managers of big enterprises to act like managers of small enterprises. A profit-center is often a snare and a delusion for other reasons, particularly if the profit-center manager does not have direct supervision of all major functions. John Dearden[8] suggests that there are limits on decentralized profit responsibility. He points out that the rate of return method of measurement may motivate a manager to achieve short-run profit accomplishments to the eventual detriment of the overall company. Thus, in complex, interdependent organizations it just may not be possible to set up meaningful subdivisions and call them "profit-centers."

In Part IV, on job design, we will discuss a means of getting individuals, at every level of an organization, to become more "profit sensible," more "profit concerned," and more "profit oriented."

5. *Build up the need for peers to accept joint or shared responsibility as a way of life.* As an organizational structure becomes larger in size and more complex in its relationships, it becomes necessary to get managers to accept joint or shared responsibility. For example, a manufacturing group and a quality control group can benefit from shared goals. There are numerous other instances in which close interrelationship lends itself to joint or shared goals. Such goals also imply a joint or shared problem-solving approach on important variances.

6. *Use policies and procedures to clarify power issues.* Recurring issues lead to the establishment of policy manuals

and standard operating procedures. It is helpful to define power issues early in the preparation of such documents. This permits these documents to state explicitly how power is to be exercised.

7. *Prepare guidelines for common positions.* In completing organization planning, it helps to identify where comparable positions exist on a given level. Illustrations might be plant foremen, plant managers, or division general managers. A guideline on the power to be exercised by such common positions should be prepared and implemented.

8. *Define precisely the power of "assistant" positions and matrix organizations.* "Assistant" positions are tricky from a power viewpoint. An assistant's power may be almost identical with that of his superior or extremely limited. Whatever the case, the top manager needs to be very deliberate about the power accorded to assistant positions.

Conflict is one of the benefits of matrix organizations. Power in a matrix organization has to be managed on a timely basis to get optimum results.

9. *Be deliberate about indirect power allocation methods.* Indirect methods of allocating power should be used very deliberately and should serve the top manager's purposes. This often means that a manager must change his personal habits. He may have to give up social and recreational practices that might result in inappropriate power implications.

10. *Keep changes in power allocation to a minimum.* There is considerable value in stability. If power allocation decisions have been made carefully, then changes in power allocation should be made very reluctantly.

11. *Check power allocations periodically.* Power is dynamic. Deliberate efforts to allocate power have to be audited periodically. In a stable organization this might be every three years.

Allocating Power in a New Structure

Let's assume that a decision to make a major change in structure has been made. It then follows that the next three elements of organization planning must be considered. Attention must be given to power, job design, and staffing. A process for allocating power in a new structure will be discussed in this chapter.

Horizontal Power Issues

The individual who occupies the top position in the new organization must resolve the power issue. This executive will need to identify where decisions about power issues are required. The first place to look at is the positions reporting directly to the top executive.

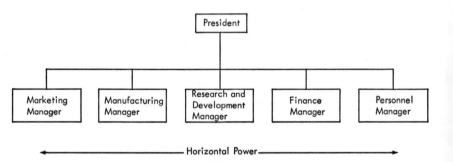

First, identify the two positions where the greatest frequency of interaction will occur. In a consumer goods manufacturing organization, as in the accompanying example, these are likely to be the marketing manager and the manufacturing manager. Then list the more important decisions which have an impact on both positions. It isn't too difficult to discover the decisions on which the most controversy is likely to occur. The alternatives for precise power allocation need to be considered. Finally, a decision on power allocation needs to be made by the top executive.

This process can be carried out by the top executive alone or in discussion with the two subordinates. The same process can be extended to other positions where there is frequent interaction until most potentially troublesome decisions have been covered.

Vertical Power Issues

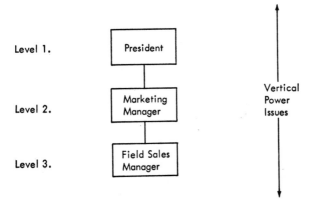

Let us next consider the relationship between the top executive, in this case the president, and the subordinate with whom he will interact most frequently. A list of important decisions which are likely to involve both parties needs to be made. Alternative grants of power need to be discussed and an agreement reached which both individuals understand and, hopefully, accept. This process permits the subject of delegation to be dealt with on an objective, operational basis. It is a rare executive whose subordinates don't feel that he should delegate more!

This process needs to be repeated with the other subordinate positions. It isn't necessary to make the list of decisions exhaustive. Once a list reflecting the vertical allocation of power exists, it is easy to add to the list as an omitted item becomes consequential.

When the process has been completed for individuals at levels 1 and 2, it can be repeated for those at levels 2 and 3. It is helpful to sum up the agreements reached in these discussions in a written document that can be used as a ready reference.

part four
Job Design

You will recall that we suggested a somewhat novel definition of organization planning in Chapter 1. According to our definition, organization planning is a systematic attempt to improve the performance of an organization by changing one or more of four elements: structure, power, job design, and staffing. Thus, in organization planning we are concerned with the behavior of an organization. In Part Two attention was given to structure as one means of insuring the desired behaviors. Part Three was devoted to power as an additional way of insuring the desired behaviors. Designing a position constitutes further "insurance." It is an important type of insurance.

What happens when a position is left ill-defined? The incumbent, of necessity, must do something. So the position is defined in terms of the incumbent's enthusiasms, interests, and anxieties. Rarely is it defined in terms of the end results to be expected. Because of this ambiguity, the odds are high that the needed behavior, the needed results, will not be forthcoming.

Recall, if you will, when you moved into an entirely new

position. Do you recall the anxiety you felt? You felt a strong
need for removing ambiguities. You first had to develop a
concept of the "job to be done." Then you had to develop
a concept of the "job well done." You had to verify that
your concepts were congruent with those of your supervisor. Job design represents a process aimed at insuring that
both supervisor and subordinate share a common understanding of the position. This common understanding benefits both
parties. The absence of such a common understanding leaves
the subordinate extremely vulnerable. One possible consequence is that the subordinate is eventually fired. Upon being
fired, the subordinate is bitter. The fairness of the decision
is questioned.

Job design is the third element of organization planning.
One might assume that devising a sound structure and then
being deliberate about power allocation would be sufficient.
But giving a title to a position is a far cry from job design!

I have found the following definition to be helpful: Job
design involves identifying the major areas in which the incumbent is expected to accomplish results and formulating
statements of the results which the incumbent commits himself
to achieve. Notice that this goes far beyond a job description.

Drucker[1] considered job design so important that he devoted an entire chapter to it in his monumental book *Management: Tasks, Responsibilities, Practices.** He argues that
the typical job description is not sufficient because it doesn't
define the specific contributions a manager is expected to
make. Drucker insightfully points out that a manager's job is
defined by relationships of mutual dependence. A manager
must contribute to his superior's success, to his subordinates'
success, and to his peers' success. The objectives which de-

---

* See bibliography for details on each reference.

fine the manager's position must have this three-way focus. Carl Lutz and Albert Ingraham[2] prefer to use the term *position management.*

The essential responsibility of any manager is to mobilize, apply, and control the resources of raw materials, facilities, money, and manpower necessary to accomplish the objectives of the organization he is managing. He must accomplish his objectives with these resources within the requirements of quality, cost, time, and legal limitations placed upon him. He must decide what mix of these resources should be applied when, where, and how to achieve the results expected of him.

"Executive strategies" involving the manpower resource concern the cost of manpower necessary to accomplish a particular objective. This cost can be expressed in the number and kinds of position needed to attain the objective. To make this determination the manager must plan, engineer, and control positions just as surely as he must plan, engineer, and control the construction and maintenance of his physical plant. This manpower segment of overall executive strategy can appropriately be called "position management."

The process of position management is beset with frustration. It can become very complicated. Because of the complexities and the general lack of understanding of the position concept, the organization and position design process in many organizations is as primitive and ill-applied as any other field of management technique. Position management fails miserably in many organizations because the managers are ignorant of its rationale.

Position management is really old-fashioned "organization planning" carried down to the individual position level. The fundamental considerations are: "Why should a position be established?" and "Why should this position be retained?"

In Part Four a chapter will be devoted to analyzing job design difficulties in an existing organization. Another chapter will describe a process for position design. Examples of position designs for a variety of positions will be found in the Appendix to Part Four.

11

Analyzing Position Definition Difficulties in an Established Organization

It was suggested in Chapter 2 that dissatisfaction with the behavior of an organization should lead to an analysis. The analysis could be done on one or more of the four basic elements of organization planning: structure, power, job design, and staffing. In this chapter we shall first consider typical position design difficulties which you will find familiar. An explanation for these difficulties will be suggested. Then five methods of analysis will be presented. They are:

1. Goal Comparison.
2. Responsibility Priority Analysis.
3. Superior-Subordinate Responsibility Analysis.
4. Intergroup Responsibility Analysis.
5. Audit of Objectives Program.

Typical Position Definition Difficulties

Each reader has been in a series of positions over a period of years. This experience provides a basis for identifying typical position definition difficulties. Compare the ones you have experienced with the ones I have selected.

Inappropriate Priorities. An individual charges off to get his job done. He strives mightily. He succeeds. But to his consternation he is criticized. He had his priorities fouled up. The results important to his boss weren't the ones the subordinate considered important.

Overlap between Two Peers. Two peers listened to the same explanation of the revised organization. One assumed he had responsibility for pricing. The second made the same assumption. The resulting conflict was serious. For some time it was defined as a personality clash. Plenty of heat was generated. But the underlying problem was faulty position design.

Gap between Two Peers. In this case each peer assumed that the other had a given responsibility. It wasn't until a "disaster" took place that this discrepancy in position definition was discovered.

Overlap and Gap between Superior and Subordinate. The same two difficulties just mentioned for peers can occur between a superior and a subordinate. Such lack of a clear and common understanding of their respective responsibilities does damage both to the relationship between the individuals involved and to the results to be obtained.

Obsolete Definition. Often an individual will retain a position title only to have a shift take place in the nature of his responsibilities and in the results expected from him. The shift often occurs gradually, over a period of years. This usually means that an incumbent carries around an obsolete concept of his position.

Inadequate Performance by a Series of Incumbents. One large company removed three successive corporate research directors. Each lasted about three years. A major contributory factor to this turnover was the lack of position definition. One research director defined the position for himself. Another waited for a definition. A third let his superior define the position. The fourth research director finally hammered out a common understanding with top management, and he hasn't been removed.

Ineffective Descriptions. Many an organization prides itself upon its position descriptions. The preparation of such descriptions represents an attempt at position definition. However, in our experience, position descriptions at best define the "job to be done." Often they don't even do this well. They seldom define when the "job is well done."

Some Assumptions about Position Definition Difficulties

The typical position definition difficulties just discussed illustrate the dynamic nature of position definition. Changes in the design of a position can occur because:

1. The superior changes his expectations.
2. A new superior arrives with new standards.
3. A subordinate's understanding of a position changes.
4. A new subordinate is appointed with a different mixture of abilities and interests.
5. External influences require that such changes be made.

In organization after organization position definition difficulties occur with great frequency at all levels.

One critical problem is to get the incumbent's understanding and acceptance of the total job. Most incumbents overemphasize the parts of the position they like and neglect the parts they dislike.

Marketing managers are stereotyped for their lack of enthusiasm for systematic planning and control. Engineering managers are stereotyped for their lack of interest in the people side of an organization.

It is a rare manager who isn't frustrated by having to spend time on long-term issues at the expense of short-term ones.

Another interesting phenomenon occurs. To use a nautical analogy, "barnacles" become attached to positions. "Barnacles" represent unnecessary work. Such work is done for various reasons—to keep busy, to maintain status, to relieve anxiety, or to avoid delegating.

Top managers in packaged goods companies often get involved in the details of an advertisement even after having approved the overall campaign plans. Some top managers skillfully divert customers' chief executives from lower-level executives who should be relating with these chief executives. Other top managers get involved with shop grievances simply because years ago they were in a position which required that they do so.

It is also interesting to see what happens when an individual steps into a new position. Few individuals take the full step. Usually a half-step is taken. Some individuals take two steps forward and one step backward. Others place one foot in their new position and leave one foot in their old position. All of this makes for a certain awkwardness.

When should a manager hypothesize that a position definition difficulty exists? The existence of an important variance between actual and expected results is an initial clue. Results, in short, are not satisfactory.

It is possible that the poor results are due to improper staffing. It is also possible that they are due to a structural or power problem. However, one hypothesis worth considering is that a common understanding of the position doesn't exist. This hypothesis can be tested quite readily. In fact, our experience leads us to conclude that the first thing to do when you are dissatisfied with a subordinate's performance is to test out the hypothesis that a common understanding of the position doesn't exist.

Methods of Analysis

Let us assume that an analysis of position design difficulties is deemed necessary. You can choose among five methods. Let us consider each method.

Goal Comparisons

A manager asks a subordinate to define his or her most important goals for the year ahead. Stress should be placed upon goals representing end *results* the subordinate believes to be important. The manager also lists the goals he expects the subordinate to achieve. A comparison of the two lists will reveal interesting similarities and differences. It may also reveal ambiguities. Thorough discussions of differences or ambiguities are needed to clarify job definitions.

An example of such a Goal Comparison follows. The superior is a group vice president. The subordinate is a division general manager. The example is restricted to ten goals be-

Goal Comparison

Division General Manager's Goals (in rank order)	Group Vice President's Goals (in rank order)
1. Achieve profit target	1. Meet or exceed profit target
2. Bring new plant on-stream on schedule	2. Reduce head count
3. Maintain adequate sources of raw materials	3. Improve on quality, reduce complaints
4. Raise prices across the board	4. Avoid raw materials shortages
5. Negotiate a competitive contract	5. Negotiate successful contract
6. Maintain good safety results	6. Bring new plant on-stream on schedule and within budget
7. Reduce head count	7. Improve on safety results
8. Maintain quality standards	8. Add depth of managerial talent
9. Increase productivity rate	9. Increase productivity
10. Professionalize managers	10. Improve team play (Manufacturing, Engineering, Marketing)

cause we have found it helpful to concentrate on a limited number of important goals. However, a second set of goals can be considered if potential benefit might accrue.

Responsibility Priority Analysis

This method is related to Goal Comparison but is not quite the same. The manager asks a subordinate to list about ten of his most important responsibilities. The superior then asks him to rank-order the finished list.

The superior then also rank-orders the subordinate's list.

Again, a comparison of the two lists bring out interesting difficulties in job definition. Discussion of the differences leads to more precise job definition. Often it is worthwhile to do both the Goal Comparison and the Responsibility Priority Analysis at the same time.

An example of a completed Responsibility Priority Analysis Worksheet follows. The subordinate is a foreman. The manager is a general foreman.

Responsibility Priority Analysis

Subordinate lists about ten of his most important responsibilities. Subordinate and manager independently assign a rank order to these responsibilities. They then discuss the differences in rank order.

Subordinate Rank	Responsibility	Manager Rank
2	1. Meet schedules	1
4	2. Produce quality product	4
1	3. Control costs	2
3	4. Improve productivity	6
9	5. Operate safely	3
10	6. Maintain employee morale	5
6	7. Improve methods	11
7	8. Maintain good housekeeping	9
8	9. Maintain equipment	8
5	10. Reduce rejects	7
11	11. Resolve grievances	10

Superior-Subordinate Responsibility Analysis

This method takes courage. The superior asks a subordinate to identify:

1. Any important responsibilities of the superior which the subordinate feels he should assume.
2. Any important responsibilities of the subordinate which the subordinate feels the superior should assume.
3. Any important responsibilities of the subordinate which the subordinate is not sure he should be assuming.
4. Any important responsibilities the subordinate feels are not getting the attention they deserve because of a lack of resources, a lack of support from the superior, or a lack of cooperation from other groups.

The superior then has a discussion with the subordinate.

An example of a completed worksheet a subordinate might bring to the discussion follows. The superior is a plant manager. The subordinate is a superintendent.

Superior-Subordinate Responsibility Analysis

Subordinate identifies:

A. Responsibilities my superior is taking that I think I should be taking.

    1. Makes decisions on work assignments of my subordinates.

    2. Makes decisions on overtime.

    3.

    4.

B. Responsibilities I am taking that I think belong to my superior.

    1. Making decisions to put employees on temporary layoff.

    2.

    3.

    4.

Superior-Subordinate Responsibility Analysis (*Continued*)

C. Responsibilities (other than B) that I am not sure I should be taking.

   1. Making decisions to change from one raw material to another.

   2.

   3.

   4.

D. Responsibilities I cannot perform well because I do not have the resources, support from my superior, or other help and cooperation that I need.

   1. Production interruptions due to faulty maintenance.

   2. Discipline undercut because Personnel is reversing my grievance decisions.

   3. Replacements of personnel not allowed even though we are below approved quota.

   4.

Intergroup Responsibility Analysis

Assume that two groups—Group A and Group B—have been selected because there seems to be some confusion as to their respective responsibilities.

Group A and Group B make a list of:

1. Responsibilites now assumed by Group B which should be assumed by Group A. (It is helpful to limit the initial set to a maximum of five.)
2. Responsibilities now assumed by Group A which should be assumed by Group B.

A confrontation discussion then takes place. Such an intergroup discussion will certainly reveal job definition differences. It can also lead to clarification and resolution of many of the differences. Occasionally, unresolved differences will have to be referred to a "higher authority."

An example of worksheets completed by Group A and Group B follows. Group A is a produce marketing group. Group B is a regional sales group.

Intergroup Responsibility Analysis

Group A

Responsibilities now assumed by Group B that should be assumed by Group A.

1. Negotiating price revisions within established guidelines.
2. Accepting returned products and granting allowances.

3.

4.

5.

Responsibilities now being assumed by Group A that really should be assumed by Group B.

1. None

2.

3.

4.

5.

Group B

Responsibilities now assumed by Group A that should be assumed by Group B.

1. Setting priorities on products to be sold.
2. Deciding who is a "major account" to be handled by central group.
3. Discussing price changes with customers.

4.

5.

Intergroup Responsibility Analysis *(Continued)*

Responsibilities now being assumed by Group B that really should be assumed by Group A.
1. Determining amount of allowances.

2.

3.

4.

5.

Audit of Objectives Program

The use of this method assumes that an Objectives Program is in operation. If it is, a periodic audit of the program can help identify job definition difficulties. The audit can explore:

1. The quality of objectives documents (specificity, results versus tasks, up-to-dateness).
2. The use made of objectives documents by the individuals to whom they apply (self-supervision).
3. The use made of objectives documents by superiors (frequency and quality of progress reviews, etc.).
4. The use made of objectives documents for team-building purposes.
5. The thoroughness of year-end accomplishment reports.
6. Opinions on the adequacy of job understanding.

Such an audit would probably be concerned with more than position definition questions. The audit can be done by either interview or questionnaire. It is helpful for a given manager to get his own data. The conduct of an audit is a contribution which Personnel can and should be asked to make for the benefit of managers.

12

A Process for Position Design

In this chapter a process for position design will be suggested. The process has proven helpful in many business, industrial, and governmental organizations. However, it might be wise to begin by examining the suggestions for position design advanced by Peter Drucker. This will permit making comparisons. It will also reveal some of the lineage of our process. Our process has evolved over a number of years. Its development has been influenced by writers on organization planning, and by managers who kept trying out our suggestions and providing us with meaningful feedback about how these suggestions worked out in actual practice.

Drucker[3] makes some interesting and helpful suggestions about the design of managerial jobs.*

1. Managerial jobs should be designed too large rather than too small. This permits those who hold them to grow, to learn, and to develop.
2. Managerial jobs should be designed to provide satisfac-

---

* See bibliography for details on each reference.

tion through performance. They should in themselves challenge and reward.

3. Worse than the job that is too small is the job that is not really a job.

4. Managerial jobs must have specific objectives, a specific purpose, and a specific function. A manager must be able to make an identifiable contribution.

5. A managerial job should combine "managing" with "working," that is, with responsibility for a specific function of one's own. The manager should be both a manager and a contributor.

6. The manager should have enough to do; otherwise he will do somebody else's work.

7. Insofar as possible, the manager's job should be designed so that it can be done by one man working by himself and with the people under his supervision.

8. The manager's job should not be designed so that he has to spend a great deal of time traveling.

9. Jobs that are "widow-makers" should be rethought and restructured. These are the jobs that defeat one good man after another without clear reasons why.

10. The design of the job has to start out with the task, but it also has to be a design that can accommodate people with different temperaments, habits, and behavior patterns.

Assumptions Underlying the Process of Position Design

It may help the reader if the assumptions underlying our position design process are stated explicitly. The reader can question the assumptions. He can also question the extent to which the process permits the assumptions to be fulfilled.

Assumption 1: A position should be thought of in terms of responsibilities for results. What are the major contributions

I should be making to the success of my organization? When one thinks about a position in this way, it is both unnecessary and undesirable to think about the position in terms of tasks, activities, or efforts. A position is not designed into a structure to do something. It is designed into a structure to help achieve objectives or overcome obstacles—two types of results.

Assumption 2: The position definition or design should be reflected in a single document. This means elimination of position descriptions. The single position document can be made to serve all the purposes of the job description and much more besides.

Assumption 3: Objectives should be "anchored" to responsibilities. A list of responsibilities provides an outline, a coatrack if you will, upon which to hang objectives. This assumption helps get the entire position in focus. It avoids the pitfall of working on a small list of high priority outcomes.

Assumption 4: The position document should be kept to a reasonable length. Long documents are difficult to prepare, hard to use, and become outdated rapidly.

Assumption 5: The position document can and should assist in the basic management processes of planning, organizing, directing, controlling, and innovating, but it should not be thought of as the document used when organization planning is done. The document should also contribute to personnel processes, such as selection, development, placement, job evaluation, salary increases, and performance appraisals. However, these contributions of the position document should not be seen as its primary purposes.

General Suggestions Pertaining to Position Design

These suggestions are admonitions to keep in mind as one undertakes the process of position design. They are also useful references when the issue of redesign arises.

Compatible Capabilities

The position should require capabilities which are likely to be found in one individual. A high degree of persuasiveness and of analytic ability are two characteristics seldom possessed by a single individual. Creative and compulsive characteristics do not usually go together.

Compatible Work Demands

The position should require compatible work demands. For example, responsibilities for long-term and short-term results should not be included in the same position if this can be avoided. It is difficult for an individual to sell two quite different products or two quite different markets with impartiality.

Complete Responsibility

Wherever possible, one individual should have complete responsibility for a given result or objective. The often recommended split between planning and doing seldom works.

Full-Time Job

The composite of responsibilities should certainly constitute a full-time job. There is merit in Drucker's suggestion that a job be made big enough to challenge and require growth. In spite of the technology developed to date, we still do not have a handle on what constitutes a day's work for a manager.

The Personality Impact

Allowances for the personality of incumbents or likely incumbents should not be made in the initial position design. Adaptations to personality can be made, if needed, when the final staffing step is taken.

A Three-Step Approach to Position Design

The three-step approach to position design involves:

a. Establishing Responsibilities.
b. Identifying Indicators.
c. Setting Objectives.

Responsibilities are brief titles which identify the major areas in which the individual holding a position is responsible for achieving results.

Indicators are the critical factors which will be examined and considered in determining when a Responsibility is well performed.

Objectives are statements of end results to be achieved within a given time period. In the three-step process, specific objectives relate to specific Indicators. The Indicators suggest the type of Objectives to be set. Only the level of desired performance has to be determined.

A typical position in manufacturing might have such Responsibilities as:

1. Costs.
2. Methods improvement.
3. Safety and housekeeping.

Examples of an Indicator for each of these three Responsibilities might be:

Responsibilities	Indicators
1. Cost	1. Actual versus standard cost
2. Methods improvement	2. Annual dollar savings from Methods Improvement
3. Safety and housekeeping	3. This year's severity index versus last year's severity index

Examples of Objectives for the above Indicators might be:

Indicators	*Objectives*
1. Actual versus standard cost	1. Actual cost 6 percent below budget for the year
2. Annual dollar savings from methods improvement	2. Savings totaling $62,000 for the year
3. This year's severity index versus last year's severity index	3. Severity index 2.3 lower for the year

Suggestions for Preparation of Responsibilities

1. Have the Responsibilities titles refer to results, not activities. (Nouns suggest results.)
2. Avoid adjectives describing a desired quality of performance. The assumption is that optimum results are mandatory. Objectives will be used to define the results expected.
3. Avoid terms that combine two major Responsibilities. Use "production volume" and "production quality" rather than "production."
4. Combine minor Responsibilities under one heading; for example, personnel (selection, development, communication, compensation).
5. Keep the number of Responsibilities of an operating type to about ten.
6. List the more important responsibilities first.
7. Add responsibilities for relationships and self-improvement to the list.

Suggestions for the Preparation of Indicators

1. List one to four Indicators for each Responsibility.
2. Make the Indicators precise, and measurable if possible.
3. Try to measure the end result, not intermediate results.
4. Where budgets or other control reports are available, reference them as Indicators.

5. Bear in mind that the "exception" is usually a more useful Indicator than the "majority."

6. Be careful about using absolute numbers. Percentages or ratios are more useful than absolute numbers; for example, profits as a percent of sales, or variance from budget versus dollars of profit.

7. Use Indicators that are important or critical to the job in question.

8. List important Indicators even if they are not readily measurable.

Suggestions for the Preparation of Objectives

An Objective is more useful if it meets the following criteria:

1. It is stated in terms of an end result, not in terms of activities or effort.

2. It is stated precisely.

3. It is measurable.

4. It is important, worthy of the superior's attention.

5. It is difficult to achieve but not unattainable.

Other Considerations in Setting Objectives

No important Objectives should be omitted even if measurement is difficult. Discussion will lead to a common concept of a "job well done."

Objectives should be stated even though the conditions necessary for success are not entirely within the subordinate's control. They never are. However, it is important that variances lead to problem-solving discussions.

We have suggested that individual Objectives need to be difficult. The sum total of all Objectives should also be challenging but achievable. The Objectives of the subordinate need to be tested against the Objectives of the superior.

Work Sheet for Preparing an Objectives Document

_____
(position)

	Responsibilities (numbers) and indicators (letters)	Objectives
1.	_____	
	a.	a.
	b.	b.
	c.	c.
	d.	d.
2.	_____	
	a.	a.
	b.	b.
	c.	c.
	d.	d.
3.	_____	
	a.	a.
	b.	b.
	c.	c.
	d.	d.
4.	_____	
	a.	a.
	b.	b.
	c.	c.
	d.	d.
5.	_____	
	a.	a.
	b.	b.
	c.	c.
	d.	d.
6.	_____	
	a.	a.
	b.	b.
	c.	c.
	d.	d.
7.	_____	
	a.	a.
	b.	b.
	c.	c.
	d.	d.
8.	_____	
	a.	a.
	b.	b.
	c.	c.
	d.	d.

Work Sheet for Preparing an Objectives Document—*Continued*

9. _____
   - a.   a.
   - b.   b.
   - c.   c.
   - d.   d.
10. _____
    - a.   a.
    - b.   b.
    - c.   c.
    - d.   d.
11. Relationships (*list any rela-tionships requiring improve-ment*)
    - a.   a.
    - b.   b.
    - c.   c.
    - d.   d.
12. Self-Improvement
    - a. Knowledge   a.
    - b. Skills (managing, other)   b.
    - c. Attitude   c.
    - d. Experience   d.

"Forcing" the Job Design

Some problems occur after a job is designed. Let's consider several.

"Old" job behaviors persist. Individuals are creatures of habit. One frequent problem occurs when a new position requires quite different job behavior. The required behavior just doesn't occur. The old job habits persist. In short, the "old" position is still in effect.

Performance is incomplete. Another problem arises from the tendency of individuals to do those things they like and to like those things they do best. A consequence of this tendency is that the incumbent, in effect, redesigns the job so that he can be successful at it. This is often done at the expense of the organization's objectives.

Concentration is often on "hot" responsibilities. A third problem has to do with the tendency to concentrate on more immediate responsibilities at the expense of more remote responsibilities.

The shift from "line" to "staff" power is difficult. Problems occur when a position is changed from one accorded the power to make decisions to one accorded the power to advise and suggest (usually referred to as a shift from line to staff). The incumbent usually finds this transition difficult and frustrating. Some incumbents don't make the change, to the confusion of the entire organization.

Some find it difficult to become "generals." An interesting problem occurs when an individual who has spent his entire career in one function moves into a general manager's position. It often takes him considerable time to find out that he has a new and different job.

These problems highlight the frequent need to take action that will "force" a position to be carried out as it was designed. Before considering ways of "forcing," let us look at methods that might minimize the need to "force" performance.

The Need for "Forcing" Can Be Minimized

1. *By proper staffing.* The more suited an individual's interests, motivations, abilities, and experiences are to a position, the more likely he will be to do the job as designed. In Part V we will take up this important problem of staffing.

2. *By effective objectives-setting.* Earlier in this chapter we outlined a three-step process for designing a position in terms of Objectives. Having an incumbent think through the

Objectives he is expected to achieve can aid in getting expected performance.

If there is reason to believe that an individual will have difficulty in doing the job as designed, it is worthwhile to increase the time spent initially in discussing the job as designed, the power allocated to the job, and the way the job fits into the organization structure.

3. *By timely training and development.* If the new position requires new skills and new knowledge, then specific plans should be made to have the incumbent secure the necessary skills and knowledge. It is important that sufficient instructional time be given in order to achieve a workable level of skill and knowledge.

In some situations, such as that of getting a potential general manager to become a "generalist," it may be necessary to anticipate this problem by a decade or more.

"Forcing" the Desired Behavior

Let us assume that the things which will minimize the need for "forcing" have been undertaken but that it is still necesary to take action to achieve the desired behavior. Here are some suggestions on how this might be done.

Make more frequent checks. Once objectives have been set, it is quite natural to provide for specific follow-up checks. For responsibilities about which more concern exists, it is quite appropriate to increase the frequency of the checks. Either verbal or written checks can be used. These checks can provide opportunities for giving encouragement and assistance.

Attach specific rewards to the new behavior. The importance of a required behavior change can be highlighted by attaching a specific reward to the change. For example, a company recently notified all general managers that their incentive pay for the next several years would be based on the performance achieved in overseas operations. A technique used by some managers is to tie a salary increase to a specific responsibility, such as the development of a stronger management team.

Provide timely criticism. There may be occasions when specific criticism is needed to "get through" to an individual that a change is needed. Many organizations hesitate to apply appropriate discipline and, as a consequence, their organizational behavior is not planned—it is allowed to evolve in a Topsy-like fashion.

Remove or redesign—a final answer. If it becomes apparent after every effort has been made that the job as designed is not going to be accomplished, then two alternatives must be faced—the incumbent will have to be removed or the job redesigned. Obviously, the merits of each individual case will dictate the alternative selected. The "art" of position design is not yet so far advanced that we can be rigid in all instances.

APPENDIX TO PART FOUR

EXAMPLES OF OBJECTIVE DOCUMENTS

Examples of Objectives documents have proven helpful to those attempting to use the Responsibilities–Indicator–Objectives method of position design for the first time.

The first example is a document for the chief executive of a multidivision manufacturing company. It is a very comprehensive document, more comprehensive than most initial documents should be. However, it illustrates the kinds of Responsibilities and Indicators appropriate for an executive who supervises autonomous businesses. It also illustrates the use of both long-term and short-term Objectives in the same document.

The second example is an Objectives document for the president of a packaged goods–type business; the third, an Objectives document for the president of a department store. Finally, a set of documents using only Responsibilities and Indicators is given. It shows the kinds of documents that are used at successive levels of a distribution organization. The hierarchy is as follows:

1. President.
2. Regional manager.
3. District manager.
4. Branch manager.
5. Salesman.

Objectives Document for Chief Executive of Multidivision Manufacturing Company

Responsibilities	*Objectives (long-term)*	*Objectives (this year)*
1. Financial results		
a. Pretax return on total assets	20 percent	17 percent
b. Pretax rate of profit on sales	10 percent	8.5 percent
c. Sales volume minimum within five years	Double	Increase 25 percent over previous year
d. Earnings per share	Steadily increasing	Increase 10 percent over previous year
e. Comparison with average of pertinent competitors	Doing as well as competitors on earnings per share	Narrow the spread by 10 percent
f. Liquidity position	Doing as well as competitors	Achieve 0.80 to 1.00 debt/equity ratio
2. Operating results		
a. Number of divisions meeting their assigned standard on pretax return on total assets	All	Meet budgeted goal for year
b. Number of divisions meeting their assigned standard on inventory turnover	All	Meet budgeted goal for year
c. Number of operating divisions which have an effective "early warning system" on operating results. (Realistic standards for operating results, timely measuring against these standards, and appropriate remedial action)	No significant exceptions in any division	All divisions have system established in all areas
d. Plant and facility inspection	No significant negatives	Set up inspection routine covering plants in each division

3. **Stability and growth**

a. Major product lines on which company has performance leadership. (Criteria: premium price, superior design, tooling advantage, superior process, reliability of product, ease of manufacturing, instances in which company has "stolen a march" on competition)	Each division will have performance leadership on 50 percent of its major product lines. Company will have leadership in no less than 75 percent of sales dollar volume	Significant improvements achieved on product lines X and Y
b. Number of established major product lines with reasonable longevity (lead time of five years on a major change)	Each division will have at least one product line with reasonable longevity	Establish basis for determination of longevity and analyze major product lines
c. Percent of volume in old product line	Not to exceed 50 percent of corporate sales	Make market study to identify major efforts needed
d. Number of major product lines in which company's share of market is maintained or improved	80 percent of total	Define and establish a system to determine market share
e. Number of marginal product lines	Marginal product lines corrected or eliminated on definite schedule	Identify all marginal lines. Work on at least one per division
f. Sales volume and profit contribution of new product effort	Corporate-wide will exceed product losses from obsolescence	Define and identify new products
g. Number of people working full time on new product effort in each division	No exceptions on number committed by each division	Every division commits to a specific number
h. Acquisition effort		
(1) Organized approach to acquisition effort	Organization, formal criteria, and procedures established	Completed and in effect

Objectives Document for Chief Executive of Multidivision Manufacturing Company—*Continued*

Responsibilities	Objectives (long-term)	Objectives (this year)
(2) Amount of exploration effort	Serious consideration (two or three meetings) given to 20 companies a year	Hit 20
(3) Actual acquisitions	On the average, two a year acquired	Acquire two
(4) Performance of acquisitions	Performed to the five-year plan developed for each division	Review results to date—indications positive
4. Managerial effectiveness		
a. Company plans (corporate objectives and goals, five-year corporate financial plans)	Prepared and utilized	Further improve on initial effort
b. Division practices and procedures (reflecting corporate policies and procedures)	Prepared and utilized	Establish and introduce procedures on major areas
c. Corporate organization structure planned	Prepared and utilized	Take no action inconsistent with basic plan
d. Precautions to safeguard assets of the company at each level of management	No important exceptions	Define and establish program
e. An improved business investment (capital appropriation) procedure	Installed and utilized regularly	Completed and in effect; further refine
f. Annual postmortem analysis of total business investment	Must hit 80 percent or better on total investment predictions	Conduct annual review—correct procedure where needed; learn from experience
g. Active and continuing cost-reduction program at corporate and divisional levels	No exceptions	Criteria and program established and working

5. *Selection, development, and motivation of key executive personnel* (key refers to people one and two levels below the chairman and president)

a.	Number of appointments made from outside company	Downward trend each year to level where three quarters of appointments are from within	Secure data and realistic goals for future
b.	Number of key positions filled with competent executives	Positive trend each year to 100 percent level	Secure data and realistic goals for future
c.	Number of choices of qualified company performers when making appointments to key positions	Positive trend each year to a standard of two internal choices	Secure data and realistic goals for future
d.	Number of "good men" who quit but could have been kept by proper handling	None	None
e.	Compensation policies and practices	Competitive on appropriate comparison (local and national)	Conduct annual review; take any action needed
f.	Number of minority employees in the management development program	At least one minority employee in an exempt position in each operating component	Specific program established
g.	Number of key managers implementing a specific effort at "professional management"	100 percent have a specific effort implemented each year	No exceptions
h.	"Fast track" (early identification) program	At least two promotions from this group each year	Establish program and identify candidates

Objectives Document for Chief Executive of Multidivision Manufacturing Company—*Continued*

Responsibilities	Objectives (long-term)	Objectives (this year)
6. *Fiscal results*		
a. Major fiscal areas meeting these criteria:	All major fiscal areas meet criteria	No exceptions
(1) Established purposes		
(2) Established practices and procedures		
(3) Planning and taking timely action		
b. Management of cash funds, credit functions, investment of funds, insurance function	No significant penalties	No exceptions
7. *Accounting results*		
a. Major accounting areas meeting following criteria at corporate, division, and plant levels	All areas meet criteria	Extend direct standard cost system to all units. Educate nonfinancial managers to understand accounting and make improved decisions
Criteria:		
(1) Established purposes		
(2) Established practices and procedures		
(3) Timely and accurate reporting		
(4) Timely and accurate records		
(5) Contributing to success of operating managers		

8. Legal

a. Managers' utilization of legal advice prior to commitment of company	100 percent	Established practices for recurring situations
b. Compliance of entire company with all legal regulations	100 percent	No exceptions

9. Industrial Relations (labor relations, wage and salary, manpower planning and development, employee benefits, selection and recruiting, safety and communications)

a. Major industrial relations areas covered by a program	All programs meet criteria	No exceptions

Criteria:

(1) Purposes established for each program

(2) Annual program proposed, accepted, and implemented

(3) Measures attempted

(4) Positive indications that purposes are being achieved

b. Number of components (a plant, for example, would be a component) judged to be "industrial relations oriented"	100 percent in satisfactory category	Set up procedures for doing this. Identify the "satisfactory—minus" components and have line managers purpose remedial plans

Objectives Document for Chief Executive of Multidivision Manufacturing Company—*Concluded*

Responsibilities	Objectives (long-term)	Objectives (this year)
Criteria:		
(1) Has its own industrial relations goals		
(2) Uses industrial relations staff resources		
(3) Places industrial relations re- sponsibility on its own line managers		
(4) Has positive programs in major areas of need		
(5) Shows indications of improved industrial relations conditions over previous year		
(6) Attitude of work force positive		
10. *Public responsibility and relations*		
a. Communications program for major publics	Criteria met	No exceptions
Criteria:		Special attention to financial public; program for improving corporate image
(1) Purposes established for each public		
(2) Annual programs proposed, accepted, and implemented		

(3) Measures attempted

(4) Positive indications that purposes are being achieved

b. Participation of key managers in community organizations (plant locations) — Top two levels participate actively

— Specific assignments made and implemented

c. Specific program for employment, development, and advancement of minority employees — At least one minority employee in an exempt position in each operating component

— Establish program

11. *Executive contacts*

a. Number of key customers known personally by corporate officers — Accomplished as planned

— Plan prepared and accomplished as scheduled

b. Number of key customers known personally by key division personnel — Accomplished as planned

— Plan prepared and accomplished as scheduled

Objectives Document for President of Packaged Goods Business

Responsibilities and Indicators	Objectives
1. *Financial results*	
a. Absolute dollar profits, this year versus last	10 percent increase
b. Pretax profit margins	Short-term: 14 percent. Long-term: 15–16 percent
c. Competitive results (margins growth)	Do better than competition
d. Trend of dollar sales per employee	Positive
e. Trend of profits per employee	Positive
2. *Growth—diversification*	
a. Full revenue sales	This year—$330 million. Five years—$700 million
b. Acquisitions in next three years	One to three which contribute $75 to $100 million
c. Number of new products market-tested each year	Minimum of three
d. Number of new products introduced nationally each year	Minimum of one
3. *Marketing results*	
a. Number of markets in which we are in a significant position (top three)	Short-term: achieve and sustain on all; action programmed on any exceptions. Long-term: no exceptions
b. Consumer image, as re-reflected in market studies	Favorable image
c. New products effort has the "thinking up front"	No exceptions
4. *Advertising*	
a. Media expenditure per share point versus competitors for market	Better than competition
b. General manager contact with evaluation of creative work	Regular contacts maintained
5. *Key personnel (Levels 1 and 2 below me)*	
a. Number of individuals "not cutting the mustard"	Any such individuals identified and a positive program established

Objectives Document for President of Packaged Goods Business—
Continued

Responsibilities and Indicators	Objectives
b. Number of men lost we didn't want to lose whom we lost due to our mishandling	None
c. "State of Union" sessions with key groups	Held on regular basis
d. Management by Objectives	Tested by me and my staff during next six months
6. Coordination with manufacturing	
a. Usefulness of customer service measurements	We stimulate a joint effort which results in getting improved measurements
b. Manufacturing variances re standards	We get benefit of having standards beat by manufacturing
c. No important delays on significant dates on promotion and new product time tables	Favorable trend; no negative situation which is repetitive
d. "Cross-bridging" of research and development and other departments	Done so "nothing falls between the cracks"
7. Personnel resources	
a. Pay and benefits re competition	Be as good as or better than competition and have people know it
b. Equal opportunity goals	Set and achieved per schedule; special attention to handicapped individuals
c. Job satisfaction "readings" taken by division and department managers	Readings predominantly positive
d. Rotation program	Accomplished as scheduled
e. Communications to employees	Annual "State of Union" for all employees
f. Action on important negative results on attitude surveys by department	Action items identified, remedial action programmed. Improvement will be shown on repeat of survey
g. Management of personnel	Do in a way so that personnel don't see need for outside representatives

Objectives Document for President of Packaged Goods Business—*Concluded*

Responsibilities and Indicators	Objectives
8. *Organization planning and effectiveness*	
a. Formal organization plans for departments and division	Implement research and development plan; periodically update others
b. Goals for number of employees	Reach goal or better it
c. Managerial controls	Pressure points study completed
9. *External relations*	
a. Personal contacts with key customers	Implement contacts per schedule
b. Trade association meetings	Secure general manager leverage advantages; customer contact by sales component
10. *Company relationships*	
a. Provision of frank, timely, and well-formulated suggestions	No exceptions
b. Represent needs of division	Provide frank representations
11. *Research and development effort*	
a. Priority given to research and development effort	Done in a timely manner; use approach which improves over last year's

Appendix to Part Four / Examples of Objective Documents

Objectives Document for President of Department Store

Responsibilities and Indicators	Long-Term (five years)	This Year
1. *Financial results*		
a. Net profit to sales (after administrative, before taxes, but excluding extraordinary charges)	5.5 percent	3.5 percent
b. Return on investment	11.0	6.7
c. Total gross margin	40.5	38.5
d. Total operating expense	35.7	36.9
2. *Merchandising*		
a. Mark-on percent	46.5	45.0
b. Markdowns	7.0	7.4
c. Turnover	4.0	3.7
d. Shortage	1.5	1.8
e. Major trends missed	None	None
f. Monthly inventory	Same as short-term	Plan not exceeded by more than 5 percent
3. *Sales*		
a. Sales projections (total, store)		Actual will meet or exceed projections
b. Sales projections on merchandise division and departments		Any poor performing areas programmed for remedial action
c. Sales per selling square foot	78.0	70.0
d. Credit business on our sales	65.0	60.0
4. *Key personnel* (selection, development, and motivation of key personnel) (two levels below president)		
a. Number of promotable men for key positions		At least one qualified internal candidate
b. Questionable performance situations		Such situations identified, specific plan set and implemented on schedule

Objectives Document for President of Department Store—*Continued*

Responsibilities and Indicators	Long-Term (five years)	This Year
c. Management by objectives program		Test out a program at top level
d. Management communication		Annual "State of Union" session
5. Operations		
a. Processing time in center (except major sale periods or storage openings)		Meet established standard
b. Central basic stock program for all stores		In operation by (date)
c. Store operating expense	19.5 percent	21.5 percent
6. Marketing		
a. Sales promotion/expense ratio	3.5	4.0
b. Marketing emphasis		Shift to more concern about profit
7. Real estate		
a. Openings	Accomplish ten openings in next five years	
b. Closings	Schedule out ahead four years (accomplish on schedule)	
c. Utilization of store space		Critical review made annually
d. Pro forma retroactive analysis		No "poor" decisions
8. Management systems and procedures		
a. Company policy and procedures manual		Upgrade, update, and issue by end of year
b. Fashion information trend system		Installed no later than (date)

Objectives Document for President of Department Store—*Concluded*

Responsibilities and Indicators	*Long-Term (five years)*	*This Year*
c. Computer applications		Schedule established and implemented
9. *Personnel*		
a. Annual performance review		Accomplished for everyone
b. Job staisfaction for all employees (know what is expected, get fair treatment, get satisfaction out of working here)		A deliberate effort made by all managers—no glaring exceptions
c. Negative working conditions		Important areas identified and corrected
d. Formalized retirement program		Issued for monthly payroll employees
e. Equal opportunity program		Specific targets set for every store
10. *Relationships* Will be set whenever an exception to effective internal or external relations is identified		
11. *Self-improvement*		Avoid working at position level below my own

Objectives Documents for Successive Levels of a Distribution
Organization

Major Responsibilities and Indicators of President

1. *Financial results*
   a. Net sales—increase over previous year
   b. Percent of gross profit on sales
   c. Operating expense ratio
   d. Operating income as a percent of sales
   e. Net profit before taxes as a percent of sales
   f. ROI before tax

2. *Operating results*
   a. Working capital control per days of sale
   b. Negotiated costs
   c. Trend of logistical expenses
   d. Selling expenses as a percent of sales
   e. Facilities and equipment utilization

3. *Growth*
   a. Of present facilities
   b. Of new facilities
   c. New products added

4. *Selection, development and motivation of key personnel (two levels below president)*
   a. Equity and competitiveness of compensation decisions
   b. Questionable performance situations
   c. Number of promotable men in key positions
   d. Relationship of rewards and performance factors
   e. On the job training for successive levels of management

5. *Business organization and planning*
   a. Business planning
   b. Regional organization structure
   c. Home office staff
   d. Basic projection process

6. *Management information for decision making*
   a. Current studies of competitive distributors
   b. Supplier attitude toward distribution in general and toward company in particular

7. *Personnel*
   a. Training and development of employees
   b. Morale of personnel

8. *Relationships (corporate or inter-company)*

9. *Self-improvement*

Major Responsibilities and Indicators of Regional Manager

1. *Financial results*
   a. Net sales—increase over previous year
   b. Percent of gross profit on sales
   c. Operating expense ratio

Objectives Documents for Successive Levels of a Distribution
Organization—*Continued*

---

      d. Operating income as a percent of sales
      e. Net profit before taxes as a percent of sales
      f. ROI before tax

2. *Operating results*
      a. Distribution expense as a percent of sales
      b. Selling expense as a percent of sales
      c. Administration expense as a percent of sales
      d. Working capital per days of sales
      e. Days sales outstanding
      f. Rate of inventory turnover
      g. Utilization of physical resources

3. *Growth*
      a. New industries and new markets
      b. New products and product lines
      c. New facilities and new locations
      d. Present plant improvement

4. *Selection, development and motivation of key personnel (two levels below regional manager)*
      a. Questionable performance situations
      b. Communications meetings with districts/branches
      c. Improvement plans for key personnel
      d. Possible replacement of personnel for key positions

5. *Business organization and planning*
      a. Business planning
      b. Regional organization structure and staffing
      c. Basic projection process

6. *Personnel*
      a. Negative situations or potentially negative situations
      b. Compensation practices—competitive
      c. Projects or programs of OSHA
      d. EOP program
      e. Education assistance program

7. *Supplier relations*
      a. Personal contact with key suppliers
      b. District/branch contacts with key suppliers
      c. Commercial intelligence

8. *Legal compliance*
      a. Compliance with company policy

9. *Relationships*

10. *Self-improvement*

Major Responsibilities and Indicators of District Manager

1. *Financial results*
      a. Net sales—increase over previous year
      b. Percent of gross profit on sales

Objectives Documents for Successive Levels of a Distribution
Organization—*Continued*

---

    c. Operating expense ratio
    d. Operating income as a percent of sales
    e. Net profit before taxes as a percent of sales
2. *Operating results*
    a. Administrative expense
    b. Distribution expense
    c. Selling expense
3. *Growth*
    a. Sales and marketing plans
    b. Expansion and better use of existing facilities
    c. New facilities
    d. New products
4. *Selection, development and motivation of key personnel*
    a. Questionable performance situations
    b. Communications meetings with districts/branches
    c. Improvement plans for key personnel
    d. Possible replacement of personnel for key positions
5. *Multiplant accounts*
    a. Primary responsibility
    b. Secondary responsibility
6. *Marketing intelligence*
    a. Customers
    b. Suppliers
    c. Competitors
7. *Personnel*
8. *Relationships*
9. *Self-improvement*

Major Responsibilities and Indicators of Branch Manager

1. *Financial results*
    a. Net sales percent increase
    b. Gross profit percent of sales
    c. Operating expense ratio
    d. Operating income as percent of sales
    e. Net profit before taxes as percent of sales
    f. ROI before tax
    g. Average invested capital
    h. DSO
    i. Inventory turnover
    j. Aged merchandise
2. *Administrative efficiency*
    a. Invoice work copies
        (1) Accuracy
        (2) Timeliness
        (3) Completeness

Objectives Documents for Successive Levels of a Distribution
Organization—*Continued*

---

    b. Credit
    c. Reports
        (1) Accuracy
        (2) Timeliness
    d. Costing
        (1) Accuracy
    e. Customer relations
        (1) Number of complaints
        (2) Back orders

3. *Personnel improvement*
    a. Employee turnover
    b. Productivity
    c. Promotable manpower
    d. Employee development—percent participating in tuition refund plan

4. *Supplier relations*
    a. Growth on supplier's line—percent increase
    b. Relationships with supplier's representative
    c. Supplier sales meetings—number of requests
    d. Turnover of business—number of referrals

5. *Market penetration*
    a. Number of new accounts
    b. New items in existing accounts
    c. Percent of market by industry type
    d. Percent of accounts sold by industry type

6. *Outside relationships*

7. *Legal compliance*

8. *Compliance with corporate/company policies*

9. *Self-improvement*

Major Responsibilities and Indicators of Salesman

1. *Sales*
    a. Percent to commitment
    b. Percent to previous year
    c. Gross profit percent
    d. New accounts
    e. New items

2. *Calls*
    a. Percent to commitment
    b. Calls on customers
    c. Calls on prospects

3. *Customer relationships*
    a. Completed calls
    b. Entertainment
    c. Personal observation (joint calls with manager)

Objectives Documents for Successive Levels of a Distribution
Organization—*Concluded*

---

4. *Records and reports*
   a. Condition and completeness
   b. Promptness in submitting

5. *Supplier relationships*
   a. Number of joint calls with supplier representatives
   b. Leads from suppliers

6. *Personal development*
   a. Commitment to improve professional selling skills
   b. Commitment to acquire more product knowledge

7. *Family relationships*
   a. Frequency of important work interference
   b. Days absent for same reason

8. *Health*
   a. Appearance
   b. Time away from job

9. *Internal relationships*
   a. Feedback from fellow employees
   b. Personal observation

10. *Expenses*
    a. Percent to sales
    b. Cost per call
    c. Selling expense/gross profit relationship

11. *Maintenance of company property*
    a. Visual inspection

12. *Self-improvement*

---

part five
Staffing

Definition of Staffing

The term *staffing* pertains to decisions as to the individuals to be assigned to given positions in the structure. *Selection* and *placement* are other terms which are often used interchangeably with the term *staffing*. A staffing decision involves matching an individual's particular set of talents with the characteristics required to perform successfully in a given position.

Comments about Staffing

Louis Allen[1] believes staffing to be important from both a financial and a human viewpoint.* He points out that in compensation alone, the career investment in an individual is a significant sum. He also notes that when you hire an individual you are investing in the happiness of both the person hired and of that person's spouse. Allen suggests that in carry-

---

* See bibliography for details on each reference.

ing out the staffing responsibility, a professional manager will give careful attention to the following:

— — His obligation to find the best people available to fill every position on his team.
— — Careful screening, against high standards, of every person accepted from another part of the organization.
— — Recommending his best people for promotion from his own group.

Allen also suggests three basic principles pertaining to selection:

1. The success of an organization over the long run tends to be proportional to the abilities of its members.
2. An individual's contribution to group objectives tends to be proportional to his ability to find personal satisfaction in the work he does.
3. An individual's past performance tends to foreshadow his future characteristics.

Typical Staffing Problems

The classical question is usually stated as follows: Should the position be designed to fit the person, or should this be avoided? One of the most frequent staffing problems occurs at this point. For whatever reason, a decision is often made to keep an individual employed in a position of a status comparable to the one he holds currently. Since this decision is often reached early in the process of organization planning, it frequently "contaminates" subsequent thinking about structure, power, and job design.

Individuals in such situations are "special treatment" cases. Normally, an individual is expected to be able to perform satisfactorily in an assigned position. But this may be a tenuous assumption as regards the "special treatment" cases. Thus "special treatment" often leads to the bastardizing of a structure designed to ensure organizational success.

A second staffing problem has just the reverse twist. The best available position isn't "big" enough to challenge the talents of a particularly capable executive.

A third staffing problem occurs when it becomes apparent that the new position calls for talent that doesn't exist in the current organization.

A fourth staffing problem occurs when an individual is to be asked to take a lower-level, lower-status position. In such instances there is usually concern about whether the demotion will be accepted.

A fifth staffing problem occurs when two quite capable candidates are competing for one position.

A sixth staffing problem is summed up by the Peter Principle. It occurs when an individual has been promoted one or two levels beyond his competence. It is interesting to observe how such a situation is dealt with. Sometimes it is ignored. Sometimes others, above or below, take up the slack. Sometimes responsibilities are shifted, positions redesigned. Sometimes a change in structure is made.

A seventh staffing problem occurs when a once competent performer becomes obsolete or ineffective.

The Importance of Staffing

Staffing is critically important to the achievement of the results expected from a position. From a structure, power, and job design point of view, a well-planned organization cannot be vitiated by a faulty appointment. Three alternatives exist in dealing with an incompetent or inadequate performer.

1. You can remove the person.
2. You can change the position.
3. You can ignore the problem.

The first two alternatives deserve serious consideration and study. Two extremes are to be avoided—jumping to a negative conclusion and refusing to face up to incompetence.

In staffing, two basic questions have to be dealt with:

1. What specifications must an individual meet to be successful in a given position?
2. Does the individual under consideration meet those specifications?

The Need to Deal with Staffing as a Process

The staffing issue can arise in an established organization. Dissatisfaction exists because results fall short of expectations. Is the incompetence of a given individual the reason? This is a basic staffing question.

The staffing issue also arises with regard to positions in a new structure. What qualifications are needed to be successful? Does a candidate have what it takes?

Both of these staffing issues need to be handled objectively and effectively. A process for handling both issues will be presented in the next two chapters.

Admittedly, a process is no guarantee of success. Sound judgment on specifications and qualifications takes more than a process.

13

Processes for Resolving Staffing Questions in an Existing Organization

Nature of the Issue

The basic staffing questions in an existing organization concern whether the individual occupying a position will be able to secure the results expected. Can he do the job? Will he do the job? Will he get the results? These are the type of questions raised. Another question often raised is the one posed by Mr. Peter's famous principle: Has the individual been promoted to his level of incompetence?

As noted earlier, staffing questions are of vital importance. How they are dealt with moves an organization toward either excellence or mediocrity. Abrupt actions and actions considered unfair encourage good men to look elsewhere. Excessive delays in moving in on incompetents also cause good personnel, usually younger ones, to look elsewhere. Let us consider two processes for dealing with staffing questions in a timely and objective manner. One process uses specifications. In effect, it repeats the appointment decision. The other process uses objectives. It tests the current reality: Have results been achieved to date?

The Specification Process

In this process the first step is to prepare specifications for the position under consideration. There is value in having a comprehensive set of specifications.

The second step is to get two or three independent judgments on whether an incumbent meets the specifications. In making such judgments, it is helpful to differentiate between specifications deemed critical and specifications deemed desirable. It is unlikely that an individual will meet all the specifications. However, he must meet the critical ones. An affirmative judgment requires that the incumbent be considered able to do the job detailed by the specifications.

The third step is for the incumbent's immediate superior to make the final decision. Often concurrence by the next higher level is required.

The Objectives Process

If the job design processes in Part Four were followed, an Objectives document will have been prepared for a given position. The evaluation of performance involves an analysis of the extent to which the Objectives were achieved. This analysis can be made once, or it can be repeated at several intervals to insure impartial and fair conclusions.

It is apparent that an established Management by Objectives (MBO) program can make a real contribution. Under such a program a subordinate commits himself to accomplish specific results, usually for a year. Once this commitment has been approved, it becomes the "contract" of the subordinate. Monthly or quarterly reviews of progress then take place. Both parties to the "contract" assess how well the objectives have been accomplished. Variances lead to problem-solving discussions and remedial action. If the variances still persist after several reviews, then both parties must face up to the reality of the situation.

If a formal MBO program is not in existence, it is necessary to establish a set of Objectives. We would recommend that the process suggested in the chapter on position design (Chapter 12) be followed. Once the Objectives have been established, an analysis of current status is made. Subsequent progress reviews serve the same purposes as those noted above for the formal MBO.

Resolution of the Staffing Question

Let's assume that the methods described above lead to a negative decision. At this point there are three choices:

1. Remove the individual.
2. Modify the position.
3. Ignore the question or postpone action.

The removal choice is a difficult one to make and to communicate. A good way to explain the choice is to review the entire analytic process that was followed in reaching it. An individual who is being removed from a position is not likely to agree with the whole analysis. However, it should be apparent to him that the process followed was both thorough and objective.

14

A Process for Arriving at Staffing Decisions

The Staffing Challenge

Again, it is necessary to recall that any organization plan is a systematic effort to achieve a change in behavior or performance.

Many well-conceived organization plans "come a cropper" when it comes to staffing. If an individual is unable or unwilling to do the job as it is designed, the benefits that can be derived from the new structure are not likely to be realized.

Placing an individual in a position represents a prediction that he will perform its duties in a satisfactory manner. This prediction requires, in effect, that three questions be answered:

1. What results are expected?
2. What specifications are essential?
3. How well does the candidate meet the specifications?

It is apparent that a well-designed job, to which specific allocations of powers have been made, constitutes an answer to the first question and aids in answering the second.

190

The Staffing Process

The staffing process begins when persons and positions are to be matched. Four steps will be helpful in improving on one's "batting average" when making appointments. These are:

1. Establish specifications.
2. Give consideration to several candidates.
3. Obtain necessary information about the candidates.
4. Compare the candidates against the specifications.

The process should begin with the positions reporting to the top manager and proceed a level at a time.

Establish Specifications

The individuals involved in making an appointment should be involved in setting the specifications.

Decide between a short-form and a long-form approach. The short form concentrates on the four to six specifications considered most critical to future successful performance. The long form may include 15 to 20 specifications. It provides more "insurance" but is more time consuming.

Specifications are usually derived from past experience. Major future changes may call for new specifications or a change in the emphases of the old ones.

Judgment in setting the right specifications comes from experience with the formal use of specifications.

Give Consideration to Several Candidates

Few candidates meet all requirements.

One's batting average improves by considering several candidates.

The best-qualified person must be qualified. The person must have a strong likelihood of being successful.

The incestuous choice of friends or protégés can be avoided by requiring consideration of "foreigners" (persons not in the immediate component). Having depth to implement this suggestion usually requires a comprehensive management development effort.

In larger organizations, personnel specialists should be expected to contribute appropriate candidates for consideration.

Obtain Necessary Information about the Candidates

Most organizations have meager information about key personnel. However, whatever information is available should be obtained (work history, performance appraisals, salary history).

Interviews of candidates who are not known personally to the interviewer can provide a good source of information. (This assumes that the interviews are done effectively; few executives have received training in interview skills.)

Reference discussions with persons who know a candidate well can also provide useful information.

Some organizations with an effective goals program do have useful data on the accomplishments of candidates.

Tests have not proven useful for selections at the managerial and executive level.

Appraisals by outside psychologists have been of help to some companies, usually smaller ones. The value of such appraisals depends primarily upon the personal skill of the individual psychologist. Most organizations should be able to secure worthwhile data without using psychological appraisals.

Here again, well-designed management development programs can provide useful data about candidates.

In some organizations personnel groups have been helpful in providing useful, descriptive information about candidates.

Compare the Candidates against the Specifications

The final step is comparing candidates against the specifications.

It helps to get more than one judgment. Independent judgments should be made before a final judgment is reached.

A Candidate Analysis Sheet facilitates comparative judgments. This form raises the three basic staffing questions mentioned earlier—objectives, specifications, qualifications.

A longer form can be used if a longer list of specifications is to be considered.

Retaining the written record of judgments about appointments permits subsequent follow-up. This is one of the best ways to improve one's ability to select talent effectively.

Candidates Analysis Procedure

Position: _____

Analysis by: _____

Date: _____

1. *Results.* List the five most important objectives the successful candidate will be expected to achieve. These should be specific and clearly measurable.

    1.

    2.

    3.

    4.

    5.

2. *Requirements.* List the five most important demonstrated abilities (skills, knowledge, experience, traits, etc.) needed for success on the job.

    1.

    2.

    3.

    4.

    5.

3. *Rating**

Candidates' Names				
Requirement 1				
Requirement 2				
Requirement 3				
Requirement 4				
Requirement 5				
Overall				
Ranking				

---

* Rating: + Fully meets requirement   √ Some reservations
        − Does not now meet requirement   ? Not sure

Candidates Analysis Sheet

Position_____Analysis by:_____Date_____

I. *Results.* List the five most important objectives the candidates will be expected to achieve.
   1. Provide a sensitive and effective "second avenue of communications" between customers and the top management of the group.
   2. Develop sufficient stature to represent the company at major conferences with customers.
   3. Upgrade the caliber of field personnel.
   4. Direct an effort to identify new business opportunities for the company.
   5. Secure and maintain the confidence of operating managers.

II. *Requirements.* List the five most important requirements for success on the job.	III. *Candidates versus requirements:**				
	A	B	C	D	E
1. Three or more years' experience as an operating manager with a record of accomplishment	1	1	3	2	5
2. Personally compatible with President and operating managers	2	1	3	3	4
3. Skillful in communications, in persuading, in establishing rapport with customers and influential persons	2	2	2	4	1
4. Capable of administering a diverse group	1	2	2	2	5
5. Sound judgment on business, political, and technical problems (across spectrum of the business)	1	3	3	3	3
Overall rating	1	2—	3	3—	4—
Ranking	1	2	3	4	5

* Rating:
   1. Fully meets, no reservations.
   2. Generally meets, minor reservations.
   3. Generally meets, moderate reservations.
   4. Generally meets, major reservations.
   5. Fails to meet.

Specification Checklist

---

1. Experience required
   a. Amount of pertinent experience
   b. Amount of supervisory experience
2. Technical knowledge required
   a. Areas requiring complete familiarity
   b. Areas requiring general familiarity
3. Education or advance training required
4. Managerial abilities required
   a. Planning
   b. Organizing
   c. Motivating
   d. Ability to delegate
   e. Ability to develop subordinates
   f. Controlling
5. Mental abilities required
6. Personal motivation required
7. Personality characteristics required
   a. Aggressiveness
   b. Judgment
   c. Emotional stability
   d. Expression (oral and writing ability)
   e. Analytic ability
   f. Self-confidence
   g. Ability to work through others
   h. Character and integrity
8. Physical requirements
   a. Health
   b. Appearance
9. Special requirements
10. Overall appraisal of promotability

General Staffing Suggestions

Previous chapters in Part V have stressed the importance of staffing decisions in an existing organization and in new structures. In this section of Chapter 14 suggestions of a more general nature will be provided.

Best Available versus Not Qualified

A frequent dilemma facing those making a staffing decision is whether to appoint the best-qualified internal candidate when it is recognized that the candidate is not qualified. At one extreme is the large manufacturing organization which prides itself on never hiring from the outside. At the other extreme is the large conglomerate which has a parade of newly hired executives. Its turnover is so fast that the internal telephone directory isn't printed any longer and the organization charts contain titles only.

Both extremes are questionable. However, a worthwhile position does seem to be that individuals appointed to key positions either be deemed qualified or be deemed to have a good chance of growing into the position.

The "They Will Quit" Pitfall

It is not uncommon for a contemplated change in structure to be slowed or stopped by the protest that key executives will quit. Have you ever kept track of the number who do quit in such instances? In our experience, not more than one in ten of those expected to quit actually do quit. True, some sulk for a period of time. It is rare that this threat is worthy of serious consideration. Occasionally, to be sure, an absolutely indispensable individual does exist. Hopefully, this indispensability is a temporary thing. If not, the organization will eventually be in serious trouble.

We would suggest that the "they will quit" prediction not be allowed to change implementation plans.

Adjusting to Personalities

We suggested earlier that individual staffing decisions not be allowed to influence structure, power, or job design decisions. However, when you do finally sit down to match talent with positions, compromise is sometimes the better part of discretion.

It is possible that, at the prevailing salary arrangement, no one is available to fill the position. If this is the case, some change in plans must be made. In some instances an individual can be found to do part of a job but may not be able to do the entire job. It is better to modify the position as designed than to ignore the difficulty. In some instances a position doesn't deserve to be at a given level, but personality considerations justify increasing the span of control. Occasionally, an individual possesses a unique and needed talent that justifies creating a special organizational arrangement to make use of this talent.

Effective Manpower Planning

To use a sports analogy, it is a lucky head coach, and usually a winning one, who can reach into his farm system for talent when he really needs it. Thus an organization with an established manpower plan, which is geared to the long-term business plan, has an advantage. In such an organization the need for talent has been anticipated. This means that the organization will have a choice among several qualified candidates when making appointments to key positions.

The need for a systems approach to executive continuity has been stressed in *Executive Continuity*, a book written by myself and William Wrightnour.[2]

part six
Follow-Through

In earlier chapters stress has been placed on analysis and design with regard to the four basic elements of organization planning: structure, power, job design, and staffing. A change can be made in any of these elements. Achieving the change requires implementation. Faulty implementation often handicaps well-designed changes.

Recently a major organization appointed an outsider as vice president in charge of a corporate staff group. The newcomer was expected to come in and turn things around. He announced that he would make some major structural and staffing changes. One month went by, a second month went by. Finally, at the end of six months the changes were announced at a large group meeting. The changes had been so long in coming that they were anticlimactic. The expected surge of enthusiasm fizzled. Several good men decided to leave.

This is an example of faulty implementation. The fault, in this instance, was excessive delay. In Chapter 15 we shall consider other examples of faulty implementation and how to avoid them.

Organizational changes, whether of structure, power, job

design, or staffing, are made on the assumption that the changes will lead to some improvement. It is therefore necessary to assess such changes. Assessment provides data on the consequences of the changes. In Chapter 16 attention will be given to means for effectively assessing organizational changes. Assessment completes the cycle of organization planning: analysis → design → implementation → assessment.

15

Implementation

Before considering suggestions pertaining to the implementation of organization changes, it will be helpful to review examples of ineffective implementation. Other examples will probably come to mind.

In one large organization the chief executive thought through a major change in structure. The change was sprung on the organization at a large meeting without any prior discussion. The organization was shocked. Those who lost out were bitter. There was little enthusiasm for the change even though many of its features were recognized as overdue. Subsequent events demonstrated that the lack of prior involvement was the critical factor that alienated the entire organization.

In another organization the pattern habitually employed in making structural changes was to appoint a task force. The task force members would talk to many individuals inside the organization. They would also talk to individuals in other companies. Eventually, a major change in structure would be announced. Interestingly, the chairman of the task force always seemed to be the person appointed to the topmost of the newly created positions. In effect, the chief executive of the organization was planning both a structural change and a staffing change at the same time. Hence it was generally assumed that the task force recommendations constituted an endorsement of the preconceived position of the chief executive. The ineffectiveness of this method wasn't due to the use of a task force. It was due to the manipulation of the chief executive. The manipulation might have gone unrecognized once, but with frequent repetition of the same tactics it became obvious to everyone concerned.

Another chief executive appreciated the value of involvement. He had long discussions with his direct reports. He used an outside consultant to insure objectivity. There were many long arguments. It eventually became apparent that these arguments occurred when the favored position was not the one the chief executive preferred. It became clear that discussion took place until the chief executive's position was recognized and endorsed. This pseudoparticipation fooled no one.

Communication pitfalls are numerous. In a modest-sized metropolitan city, executives at one company were dumbfounded at the speed with which organizational announcements got out. On several occasions irate wives would call their husbands because a local real estate agent had called to say he had heard from a good source that their house was to be put on the market. Upon questioning his superior, the bewildered spouse would find, to his amazement, that there was a strong likelihood that he would be asked to move.

Major structural changes are often announced at a large group meeting. A disastrous slipup occurred at one meeting of this kind. The entire group of executives of a large manufacturing organization was brought together to meet with the chief executive. The chief executive assumed that everyone in the audience had been given a written announcement of the changes. So he began by asking whether anyone had any questions about the announced changes. He took the subsequent silence to mean that there were no questions. Afterward it took considerable scrambling to brief everyone.

Announcements at large group meetings are often characterized by a rather resolute avoidance of questions. Certainly no real "zingers" are going to be tossed out on these occasions. So such sessions usually result in a one-way flow of information.

These examples do not exhaust the possibilities for ineffective implementation. You may add others from your own experience. But the examples do illustrate an important fact —effective implementation is of real importance. The assumed gains from a sound organizational change may be lost entirely due to faulty or ineffective implementation.

Let us now turn our attention to six implementation suggestions. They will have to do with:

1. Involvement.
2. Timing.
3. Communications.
4. Use of titles.
5. The organizational manual.

Specific suggestions pertaining to the above categories follow.

Involvement

It has been stressed that the organization structure is a tool of the top manager. While this is true, those at lower levels are also directly involved. Their attitude toward a change in structure can have a big effect on getting the desired changes in behavior or performance.

The involvement of those affected is very worthwhile in securing understanding and acceptance of decisions. The methods mentioned in the chapters devoted to the analysis of the four organizational elements provide for full involvement.

A manager can involve his immediate staff. He can use a task force to involve several levels. As the organizational planning process "cascades" down the organization, each manager can involve his portion of the organization.

Timing

The timing of organizational changes is of significance. Let's first consider structural changes. The process to be used, as recommended in Chapter 7, results in what can best be called a long-term structure, one that is likely to be in existence five years hence. Sometimes the ideal organization is deemed worthy of immediate implementation. Sometimes timing considerations may require a phased evolution from the current structure to the ideal structure. The phases can be scheduled on a tentative basis. The timing decision needs to take into account such factors as the prevailing economic climate. It is best to avoid making a major structural change during an organizational crisis. Such a crisis may be due either to a recession or to a rapid expansion.

The timing of changes in power and job design is less critical. Such changes can be made whenever an analysis shows them to be necessary.

Staffing changes present interesting timing issues. The prevailing tradition of the organization will probably govern. Some large enterprises are well known for their abrupt dismissal of executives. Others are known as very deliberate.

They "take care of" their executives, arrange moves to other positions, "save face."

Communications

A structural change calls for rather precise timing of the relevant communications. The individuals affected by the change are entitled to a personal explanation from their superiors. Immediately thereafter, all other individuals who have a need to be informed should be informed. A group meeting or a series of group meetings is usually needed. Experience suggests that the following sequence is likely to be most effective:

1. A full explanation of the structural change is given.
2. The large group is divided into smaller groups to generate questions.
3. Questions are reported to the entire group and classified into major categories.
4. Full answers are given to questions by category.

There is a tendency to exaggerate the potential benefits of a change in structure. This should be avoided. It leads to excessive expectations.

Communications on job design and power changes do not usually require formal sessions, though the analytic process described in earlier chapters usually requires involvement. Confirmation of decisions on changes is the prime needed communication.

Use of Titles

An organization can use a title for one or more of the following purposes:

1. To inform persons both inside and outside the organization of the general nature of the contribution expected of a position.
2. To designate the organizational level of a position.
3. To show that the incumbent of a position is an officer of the company and/or a subdivision.
4. To designate the geographic location of a position.
5. To indicate the reporting relationship of a position.
6. To provide the status the occupant of a position needs in order to establish effective external relationships.
7. To indicate the managerial or supervisory responsibilities of a position.

Titles used in these ways facilitate communication.

Titles have two types of values. One is functional. The other is emotional or motivational. A title often fulfills an individual's need for status. Some individuals have extremely strong status needs; some do not. Status needs may operate inside and outside an organization. Such needs are often shared by the individual's spouse.

The most widely prevalent pattern for dealing with titles can well be called *haphazard*. Under this pattern a growing company exercises little control over organizational titles. The situation usually gets out of hand when several acquisitions are made. The major disadvantage of the haphazard approach is that it does not achieve the communication value of titles. In addition, the haphazard approach is guaranteed to have an adverse impact upon morale and motivation.

A second pattern is that of rigid standardization. The most vivid example of this was General Electric in the mid-50s. The GE hierarchy then went from president to group vice president to division general manager to department general manager. Each department general manager had five positions reporting to him—manufacturing, marketing, engineering, finance, and employee relations. No "assistant to" or "assistant" titles were permitted. Title guidelines extended to nonsupervisory personnel. For example, restrictions were placed upon the use of the title "engineer." This pattern represented a considerable amount of "overkill." It avoided the pitfalls of the haphazard approach. However, its rigidity also made it difficult to organize to meet the changing needs of quite diverse businesses.

A third pattern might be called the "nomenclature guideline" approach. A well-stated guideline is issued to key managers. They can use any titles they wish if the titles are consistent with the guidelines. Exceptions have to be cleared with an assigned top-level corporate component. This third pattern, in our opinion, avoids the extremes of the other two. Its use means that titles will be employed constructively as a "management tool."

Obtaining a title often fulfills a need to achieve, to progress, to "climb a mountain." Some individuals appreciate a title because it gives them power, and this is of great concern to them. Thus it is that titles can be used to attract talent and to motivate achievement. Titles can also be used as one of many means by which to retain talent.

The Organizational Manual

There is a need to issue a formal reference that reflects the design decisions on structure, power, job design and staffing. This reference is usually called an Organizational Manual. The manual usually includes organizational charts reflecting the intended structure and staffing.

The position design process will result in an Objectives document. This can be made a part of the Organizational

Manual. Formal statements concerning power, such as authority documents, can also be included in the Organizational Manual.

Impact of Organizational Planning on Other Functions

It is interesting to note that a change in organization structure calls for many other changes. Usually the splitting or merging of major components requires that the accounting fraternity revise the basis for financial reporting. This is often done on a retroactive basis to provide needed comparisons.

16

Assessment

Assessment is another follow-up requirement. *Assessment* is the term used for a thorough study of the outcomes of an organizational change. The assessment steps close the loop, which began with analysis, then shifted to design, and then to implementation.

In many organizations one sees a pattern of quick changes and quick assessments. The somewhat predictable pessimistic conclusions of the quick assessment that follows a quick change lead to another cycle of quick change and quick assessment. We would argue that this circular process is both uneconomical and demoralizing.

In this chapter attention will be given to the timing and technique of assessment.

Timing Assessment

There is a fallacious tendency in some organizations to make a change today and to assess its consequences a month later. The following rules of thumb for timing assessment vary by size of organization. The larger organization will need a longer period of time before attempting assessment.

Considerable experience suggests that the following timing of assessment is appropriate:

Major change in structure: 1 to 2 years.

Minor change in structure: $\frac{1}{2}$ to 1 year.

Significant change in power allocation: 1 to 2 years.

Change in staffing at several levels: 1 to 2 years.

Change in staffing in positions at the same level: $\frac{1}{2}$ to 1 year.

Changes in job design: 6 months.

Structural Changes

A major structural change is a significant shift from one organizational alternative to another at the level reporting to the top manager. Examples of major changes in structure include the change from a functional to a product-type structure, from a product-type to a geographic structure, from a functional to a matrix structure.

In our experience, at least a year must go by before the real effects of a major structural change can be seen. Making new appointments and transmitting communications about the change occupy the better part of a month. Then the entire organization has to go through at least one entire business cycle before a serious assessment of the change is begun.

A minor change in structure might be to combine two positions or to split one position reporting to the top manager. The results of such a change should become available to assessment in six to twelve months.

Power Changes

A significant change in power can be said to occur when one of the direct reports is accorded new authority, or when managers at an entire level are granted important new power.

We see a need to let the new arrangement "percolate" for a year or more before making an assessment.

Staffing

If staffing changes are made at two successive levels of an organization, in our experience the shakedown takes about one year. Thereafter it should be possible to assess results after six to twelve months.

Job Design

Changes in job design can be assessed effectively after six months.

Assessment Alternatives

The assessment process has been covered in previous chapters. Chapter 3 provides a process for analyzing an existing structure. In assessing a new structure we would first reconstruct the objectives and obstacles which were used in designing it. Were the objectives achieved? Were the obstacles overcome? An affirmative answer would not prove that the new structure was right, but it would probably give one sufficient confidence that you would not devote much more time to assessment.

Let's suppose there is a significant negative variance from objectives. The question then is whether this is due to faulty organization structure, faulty power allocation, faulty job design, or faulty staffing. To make your determination we would suggest that you begin by following the process suggested for analyzing a current structure in Chapter 3. If this doesn't ring a bell, shift to the process given in Chapter 9 for analyzing power problems in an existing organization. If the negative variance still isn't accounted for, shift to one of the processes suggested in Chapter 11 for analyzing position definition difficulties in an established organization. If that doesn't do the trick, use one of the processes given in Chapter 13 for resolving staffing questions in an existing organization.

If the negative variance cannot be accounted for as you complete these processes, you can begin to look for the villain in areas other than organizational planning.

part seven
Special Issues

Extensive experience in planning organization structure at the top executive level suggests that a special approach is needed at the very top. The processes described for dealing with structure in earlier chapters do not meet the complexities at the top of the pyramid. Chapter 17 is devoted to a practical approach for organization planning at the chief executive level.

An extensive study of the construction industry permitted us to study the evolution of relatively small organizations. A report on the stages of evolution we discovered in the construction industry is included in Chapter 18. At each stage attention is given to four behavioral phenomena:

— –top management work.
— –top management worries.
— –top management processes.
— –the critical requirements for top management success.

This study provides further illustrations of the behavioral aspects of organization planning.

17

Organization Planning at the Chief Executive Level

The "top of the pyramid" presents some unique challenges when it comes to organization planning. The Conference Board[1] periodically studies the trends in organization planning.* A recent study at the executive level identified four major trends in large companies:

1. A greater divisionalization accompanied by decentralization.
2. The elaboration of the corporate staff and changes in its role.
3. The emergence of group executives.
4. The elaboration of the chief executive's office.

The greater divisionalization was attributed to expanded product lines, a wider variety of markets, difficulty with the assignment of responsibility for profits, and a need for greater flexibility.

The changing role of staff revealed a truism. As a company grows, staff also grows. This mushrooming was found to be due to the need to service large numbers, to internal re-

---

* See bibliography for details on each reference.

sourcing, and to the provision of quite new services. Governmental regulation, for example, had spawned numerous new staff groups.

The role of staff at the corporate level was seen as shifting from service to assisting in planning and controlling. In a sense, staff become custodians of corporate integrity in divisionalized companies. The emergence of corporate staff as a major force has been characterized as "recentralization" —as a reaction to too much decentralization.

The group executive's role was seen as emerging because of the proliferation of product divisions. This position reduces the chief executive's span of control. It provides closer supervision and control. The responsibilities and authority of group executives are not always clearly defined.

The previous three elements can be viewed, says the Conference Board, as means used by chief executives to manage a growing and far more complex business; all three allow the chief executive to devote more of his time to the responsibilities uniquely reserved to him.

> It is evident from the organization structures in this study that companies—or more particularly, chief executives—are using several methods to cope with the expansion of the reserved responsibilities of the chief executive. All the methods elaborate the office of the chief executive so that these reserved responsibilities—"the chief executive function"—are being performed by more than one man. Accountability still rests with the chief executive officer alone, but the function, it might be said, is "decentralized."
>
> Another method that appears quite frequently among the participating companies amounts to an upgrading of the president–executive vice president relationship. An increasing number of companies are allocating the chief executive function to a chairman of the board designated "chief executive officer." The president in these companies is sometimes designated "chief operating officer," or sometimes "chief ad-

ministrative officer." In some companies there is a definite split in responsibility of the two men, but quite often they "share the same box" and share responsibilities.

In a very few of the participating companies, not just two but three (a chairman, president, and an executive vice president) and even four men (a chairman, president, and two executive vice presidents) share this top box and the duties of the chief executive.

Still another method of coping with the increased complexity of the chief executive function calls for the creation of a council of top executives to carry out this chief executive function. The concept involved here cannot be adequately depicted on any chart. But a few companies use a special charting device to emphasize the idea. One box labeled "executive officer" or "executive management" or "office of the president" appears at the top of the chart. It includes not only the chief executive and the executive vice president(s) but also those group executives and general staff executives accountable for coordinating the operating and corporate staff components of the business.

Organization of the Chief Executive's Job

The Conference Board identified several prevailing patterns of organization of the chief executive's job as illustrated in patterns 1–5.

Organization Planning Applied at the Top

Long observation of organization planning applied at the top level of enterprises leads me to suggest that the logical processes proposed in this book be ignored by the newly appointed chief executive. The newly appointed chief executive should think through how he personally wants to operate. The basic choices are four in number:

Pattern 1

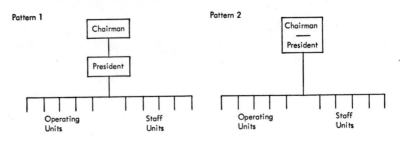

Pattern 2

Pattern 3

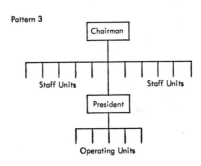

Pattern 4

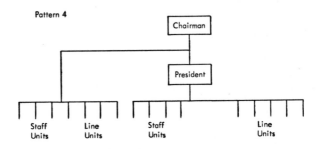

Pattern 5

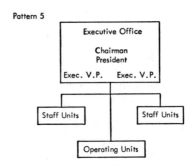

1. To run his own show.
2. To set up a partnership consisting of either two senior partners or a senior and a junior.
3. To set up a troika with some division of labor.
4. To set up a quartet with assigned hegemonies.

Interestingly, size doesn't seem to make any difference. It is fine for Drucker to argue that large enterprises can't be run by one person. I wholeheartedly agree with his position. That doesn't keep many an executive of large enterprises from at least trying to run a one-man show.

An abrupt staffing change was made by a newly appointed chief executive of a major newspaper. The new chief executive was an outsider, but he had had a very comprehensive briefing on the problems of the organization. On his very first day he called in the 12 executives who reported to his predecessor and fired every one.

Did he act too soon? We don't know yet. The evidence after six months is that this was a masterful stroke.

It doesn't seem to help to suggest that one approach is more relevant in a given industry. It is well known that several very large oil companies are dominated by one individual, whereas others are run by the consensus of several individuals if not by a committee.

I have about concluded that a new chief executive can only be influenced to make up his mind as soon as possible and to get on with his decision. The decision is primarily an emotional one. Some of the motivational pressures are available for analysis; some are not. One chief executive was rebuffed by a subordinate soon after being appointed. He removed the subordinate immediately and then reviewed the scene for other potential threats. He singled out three, assigned them to the office of the chief executive, and gave them no power. Thus he neatly eliminated the possibility of future threats.

In our terminology, he dealt with a potential power problem. True, the salaries paid were enormous, the frustration generated was high, and the enterprise suffered because it was too large to be run by one person. But the chief executive stayed with this arrangement up to his retirement. This might well be an example of the use of the chief executive office as a means of obfuscating accountability.

A chief executive has built up long habits of working with others before he gets to the top. Factors which are going to influence the structure decision at the very top are:

1. How much the chief executive trusts others.
2. How much exerting power means to the chief executive.
3. The extent to which the chief executive can share power.
4. The extent to which the chief executive can share the limelight.
5. The self-confidence of the chief executive.
6. The assumptions made by the chief executive of threats to his position.

We are beginning to see boards influence decisions. Boards are encouraging chief executives to change their habits. The *Wall Street Journal* and other business publications quite often report upon chief executives who are being pressured by their boards to stop being one-man shows and to share some of their power. This is certainly an appropriate role for a board.

This issue of organization at the top suffers because of a tradition, rooted in our rugged individualism, that several candidates should be competing down to the wire for the top spot. The one competitor appointed is a winner, and the remaining competitors are losers. Psychologically, it becomes quite difficult for the competing candidates to become a close-knit team.

In large enterprises, the problem of executive succession should be viewed as that of developing a team who will be put in place. The team might well be tested for compatibility early. The exact titles might well be resolved by chance. Obviously, the talents of the team would be complementary.

18

Stages in the Evolution of Organization in the Construction Industry

The construction industry provides interesting insights into the evolution of organization as a very small company changes into a middle-sized company. A study of numerous construction companies reveals key stages in the evolution of the organization structure.

Stage 1   begins with the founder. The organization is run by a single, dominant individual.

Stage 2   involves the establishment of a two-man or possibly a three-man group at the top. As often as not, one is the son of the founder. The son has gone to college and studied engineering.

Stage 3   sees the arrival of a general manager at the top with a strong functional level of management now in place. At this stage, the son usually takes over the reins.

Stage 4   sees a level of general managers or profit-center managers reporting to the top executive. A small central staff and multibusiness units are the pattern.

Let's take an intensive look at the way the organization

behaves at each stage from the viewpoint of the top manager. We will consider four behavioral aspects:

1. Top management work.
2. Top management worries.
3. Top management processes.
4. Critical requirements for top management success.

A feel for the evolution of the organization is provided by a consideration of top management work and worries at each stage.

Stage One

Top Management Work

At Stage 1 the top manager makes all the decisions. He makes them quickly. He selects all supervisory and many of the nonsupervisory personnel. The top manager keeps track of all work in progress on each project by personal visits, usually on a daily basis. He sets the standards for all the work. He can do this because he started as a craftsman himself. He personally motivates the workers. He commands their respect because they know he knows his trade. The top manager spends time running the company, but he doesn't call it management. In an emergency he jumps in and becomes a craftsman again. Stage 1 projects tend to be on the small side and of short duration.

Top Management Worries

Worries at Stage 1 are primarily about short-term results. Schedules must be maintained, costs must be controlled. The top manager usually considers these minor worries. His serious worry is that he is getting older and realizes that he cannot continue to run the company much longer. By this time he has reached an unexpected state, namely, that of being wealthy. A son is likely to be graduating from college, and the father worries about him. There is an ambivalence. He needs a successor; this young whippersnapper is educated, but he doesn't know any trades. Will he really be able to fill the old man's shoes? That's the worrisome question.

Another worry is being away from the business for even a day. Things don't really seem to go right unless the top manager is there. He wants a replacement "in the wings," but he doesn't want the replacement to make decisions. However, the projects get larger. Success begets more success. Reluctantly, the top manager finds himself being pushed into Stage 2.

Top Management Processes

Supervisory routines are casual. The top manager assigns work, follows up on it, and both rewards and punishes. He signs everything. He may even open the mail. Planning and reporting methods are primitive. They are a step ahead of the "back of the envelope" period. There are no staff meetings. Contacts are on a one-to-one basis. Control is exercised by personal inspection. Limited use is made of records and reports. Formalities are shunned—there are no job descriptions, organizational charts, standard operating procedures. The manager provides motivation by setting an example of hard work and by direct, blunt comments. He spends very limited time thinking very far ahead. It has been said of a manager like this, "He can manage what he can see!"

Critical Requirements

At Stage 1 the top manager must know every aspect of the business. He must have intimate knowledge of bidding, scheduling, production, accounting, labor. He must be capable of doing the more critical work himself. He must be able to plan the work, assign it, and follow up to get desired results. He must be able to motivate personnel either by fear or by leadership, and he must have the stamina to work long hours, often in adverse weather.

Starting one's own enterprise requires strong drive, a desire to run one's own show, and a willingness to take on responsibility. Individuals meeting the foregoing requirements are usually referred to as "real" entrepreneurs.

Stage Two

At Stage 2 the top management of a construction enterprise consists not of a single entrepreneur but of two or possibly three men. The organization is two to four times as large as it was at Stage 1.

Top Management Work

At Stage 2 the work is basically the same for top management as it was at Stage 1. However, it is now shared by two or possibly three men. The assignment of responsibilities is rather casual. Usually the older top manager takes on the responsibility for being Mr. Outsider, directly supervising projects. A Mr. Insider takes on the work of bid preparation, record keeping, and similar chores. The projects are much larger and take much longer. Competition is such that the risk of losses increases greatly.

Top Management Worries

Worries about project performance still exist. Maintaining control of schedules and costs becomes more difficult as the projects get larger. New methods, such as computers, are introduced by the younger top manager. The founding top manager worries because the younger top manager manages so differently. He doesn't visit projects daily. He doesn't impose standards. He trusts reports and records.

The need for a successor becomes much more acute. However, the younger men seem to be somewhat "light" for such responsibility.

Often another worry arises. The key managers begin to imply that they should be cut in on a piece of the action. Their expectations are worrisome because, in the eyes of the founder, they are so unreasonable.

During Stage 2 one or more disasters occur. A project loses money. Often lots of money. This adds an acute concern to the worry of controlling to avoid future disasters.

A new worry occurs. Up to this point the business just evolved. Projects involved the same work, scaled to a larger scope. Now it becomes necessary to question whether one should stay local. If one is to stay local, then it will be necessary, it seems, to expand into other business lines. A business line, in construction, might be sheet metal work, plumbing, bricklaying, foundation work, erection work, etc. A second choice is to stick to one's specialty but to expand geographically.

Here are the classic alternatives discussed in Chapter 6. There is a real pressure to grow. However, moving into new types of work or new territory involves risk. It now becomes necessary to break with past tradition. The top two or three managers rarely see eye to eye on the changes. The older top manager is usually reluctant to change at all. The younger men often want to charge off in several directions at the same time.

Top Management Processes

The top management processes are still on the informal side. They may not be quite as casual as those of Stage 1. The biggest change is the opportunity to subdivide the top management position. One top manager may become Mr. Outsider, another Mr. Insider. Usually the older top manager takes on the responsibilities he likes, leaving the remaining responsibilities to others. The new, younger managers come out of engineering school or business school with an enthusiasm for management methodologies. They push for data processing, organizational charts, and other systematic management methods. Gradually, these are incorporated into the enterprise as Stage 2 evolves.

Critical Requirements

The requirements for Stage 2 have not changed much from those for Stage 1. However, several changes are under way. The organization is becoming larger and more complex. If the company moves into new businesses or new territories, these new areas have to be mastered. In addition, the one-man show has now become a two- or three-man team. The initial one-man executive now gives way. Two or three executives must be both able and willing to work together. This gets quite interesting when the father-son variation is added to the equation. In the latter part of Stage 2 the differences between father and son become extreme. The usual resolution sees the father deciding to retire and turn the entire business over to the younger generation. This usually occurs five years before the father wanted it to and five years later than the son wanted it to.

Stage Three

Stage 3 sees a top management group of two to three with a strong level of managers reporting to them. The business is either multiline or multilocation.

Top Management Work

A significant change has now occurred. Much of the top management work done at Stage 1, and also at Stage 2, has now been pushed down to the strong superintendent level of management. Top management now spends more time on the important political aspects of the business. Business decisions, particularly bids and bid parameters, are now very complex and critical. A major bid amounts to "bet your company." IBM may "bet the company" on a 360 computer line introduction once in a decade. The typical construction management "bets its company" several times a year.

Top management now reviews and passes on important recommendations of the general superintendents. As conflicts arise, top management makes the crucial trade-off decisions. Top management now faces the task of attracting, selecting, motivating, developing, and retaining a competent superintendent level of management. It devotes attention to getting team play.

Top Management Worries

The primary worry is whether the construction work will be performed satisfactorily without top management's close personal involvement. The top manager worries when he doesn't delegate and also worries when he does. He worries about a superintendent who doesn't measure up. He also worries about the future growth of the business. He feels strong pressures to continue in the growth tradition. At the same time, he worries about overhead costs and a reduced rate of profit.

By this stage numerous "modern management methods" have been introduced. Top management now worries about how to make them work, how to get them to pay off.

Top Management Processes

The top manager or managers now begin to spend their time managing. All important decisions are still made at the top, but the successful accomplishment of day-to-day results is delegated to lower-level managers. Planning becomes more formal. Department heads commit themselves to target dates, to specific results. Top management now gets regular written and verbal reports by which to control. Personnel policies and procedures are developed to achieve more uniformity. Recurring problems are also covered by policies and procedures. Department heads are brought together for staff meetings. Anytime a critical problem develops, the top manager gets involved with it personally. Some attention is devoted to the development of personnel. By this time the top manager has discovered that he doesn't have to sign everything.

Top management begins to add staff individuals or groups to help it manage the enterprise. A controller is added, then a personnel manager.

Critical Requirements

The individuals in top management positions must really become managers. The ability to delegate becomes essential. The ability to develop and select competent department heads is vital. Skill in establishing and utilizing central staff contributions becomes an important requirement. The top managers have to be knowledgeable about every major function so that optimum results can be secured from each function and timely trade-off decisions made.

Formal planning skills have to be developed. The ability to set up and use a reporting system for control is also necessary. Skill in effective two-way communication becomes essential. Being able to identify and exploit business opportunities is a vital necessity.

Stage Four

Stage 4 leads to an organization with a top management group, central staff groups, and autonomous business entities. The business entities have their own resources and are held to a profit and loss responsibility.

Top Management Work

Top management work now involves making policy decisions on business direction, business objectives, and resource allocation, and establishing guidelines for the decision making of subordinates. Top management now selects general managers who set up and use a planning and reporting system to maintain control. The corporate staffs are used to help maintain control, stimulate excellence, and perform "pooled" work. Integration to get hoped-for synergism is a responsibility of top management. Top management must also resolve conflicts on business scopes or charters.

Top management, usually after getting burned, sets up a system for detecting exceptions to expected results so that quick corrections can be made.

The company begins to take on very big jobs. Top management now spends time developing strategies for getting big jobs. It becomes part of "multiple level" selling.

The nature of top management's work has become quite different at Stage 4 than it was at Stage 3. Directing general managers and utilizing a central staff group require what might be called the ability to manage an institution. At Stage 1 the top manager directed actual work and sometimes performed it. Interestingly, the son often criticized his father for not making the transition from Stage 1 to Stage 2. Now the same son often has difficulty in making the transition from Stage 3 to Stage 4.

Top Management Worries

Top management now worries about which expansion philosophy to follow. Should we move into new lines of business or new geographic markets? Top management becomes concerned about general managers not being as big, broad, and deep as desired. They become concerned about other key men who have become obsolete and about action needed to have successors come along.

Top management now worries about pesky smaller competitors and continued pressure on profit ratios. It seems to top management that more and more risk is required for less and less gain.

Top management now worries about conflicts between operating divisions and central groups. It also worries about the utilization of available resources, such as equipment, finances, and personnel.

The top managers now endeavor to discover the critical elements making for success in each business line or each geographic area so they can worry about the things that really count.

Top Management Processes

The former top management work is now pushed down a level. The new and different top management work requires new management processes. Everything becomes more systematic. Policies and procedures blossom into a big manual. Objectives, one- and five-year forecasts, and budgets are required. Special inspection and audit processes are initiated. Formal review processes are set up. New financial reward systems are developed to motivate those in the respective businesses to do their best.

The reporting system is standardized. It increases in complexity. Complex computer systems are used. Chart books for control are developed. The reporting system gets more complex each time top management is surprised. As the size of the work force increases, the personnel staffs increase. Personnel procedures and programs are initiated in a more formal way.

Critical Requirements

A most critical requirement is that the men in top management see themselves as managers of general managers. Most of their former work has to be pushed down a level. Guiding several managers in their respective businesses requires working on a different time perspective. The ability to plan longer term becomes critical. The ability to give business managers considerable freedom, and then not to be surprised when a project gets out of control, is vital.

The top managers must develop a knowledge of the elements critical to the success of each business line and/or each geographic area and then learn how to control these elements. They must be able to act and interact effectively on governmental and political issues.

Implications for Organizational Planning

A study of an admittedly small number of construction organizations has led us to the following observations about the transition from stage to stage in the construction industry.

1. There is a time lag of about five years in moving from stage to stage. It is the failure to make the necessary

changes in habits, structure, and methods that constitutes this lag.

2. It is extremely unlikely that the founding entrepreneur, who did everything at Stage 1, can be effective in building and managing the much bigger enterprise of Stage 3.

3. Family firms react more slowly in moving from stage to stage than do nonfamily firms. The necessary changes usually have to wait until the new generation takes over.

4. Several symptoms of a lag in moving to the next stage are:

    a. The top manager works harder, but overall operating results deteriorate.

    b. Fire fighting becomes habitual for the entire organization and is even accepted as a way of life.

    c. Other competitive organizations begin to make inroads. They also produce superior financial results.

    d. The top management has grown old together.

5. The critical requirement in moving from Stages 1 and 2 to Stages 3 and/or 4 is one of attitude. The top manager must change his concept of himself. He must worry about different things. Above all, he must get new and different satisfactions out of his position.

6. Some difficulties encountered in the evolution through successive stages have been reported by numerous executives in construction enterprises. They are:

    a. The loss of a chance for the top manager to have face-to-face contact with the workers and first-line supervisors.

    b. Difficulties in getting information up and down the "line."

    c. Executive isolation and the screening of executives from reality.

    d. A loss of entrepreneurial spirit.

    e. The danger of rigidity and red tape.

    f. Difficulties in determining what the top job is and how to organize for it.

    g. Difficulties in exercising effective control.

    h. Difficulties in maintaining employee morale.

    i. The failure of old solutions and old ways of doing things to meet the needs of the expanded operations.

7. The economic trends in the industry and in specific parts of it are critical in determining when a shift to a new stage should be made. There isn't any magic answer about the size for a given stage. Each individual has to use a combination of facts and intuitive judgment in arriving at a decision to move to a new stage. Exchange of experience with other executives in the industry helps one calibrate where one's organization is and where it should be.

8. A serious delay in moving to the next stage in development can jeopardize the future of a firm. It almost inevitably leads to adverse financial results. In some instances it can lead to the demise of the enterprise.

9. Some assumptions about the construction industry:

    a. It is unlikely that acquisitions will be available at a reasonable cost.

    b. It is unlikely that competent management will be found in an acquisition. Most acquisitions are firms at Stages 1 and 2.

    c. Costs, such as those for materials and labor, will continue to increase. Becoming astute in all aspects of managing is one remaining way to secure a competitive advantage.

    d. Critical to success in a geographic area is an effective working relationship with the trades and with subcontractors.

e. It is important to decide not only what business lines to be in, but also what business lines not to be in. There are advantages to concentrating on a limited number of business lines, lines in which one is competing from strength.

f. It is vital to organize and manage for timely control over costs.

g. It is absolutely essential to restrict critical risk decisions to top management.

h. In the construction business you can't get well in a hurry, but you can get "sick" rapidly.

i. Money spent on getting a good topflight management team does not produce the same leverage as it would in a manufacturing organization.

j. Small organizations, in fact all enterprises at Stages 1 and 2, have a difficult time developing successors for top management positions.

The above review of the evolution of organization in the construction industry suggests that it is possible to identify at least four basic stages in the evolution of organization structures. The stress we place on looking at organizational planning from a behavioral viewpoint is vividly illustrated by the changes which occur at each stage with regard to top management's work, worries, processes, and requirements. It becomes apparent that the persons in top management have to change. The shift from Stage 1 to Stage 2 may not be great, but the shift from Stage 1 to Stage 3 is drastic. Similarly, the shift from Stage 2 to Stage 4 is drastic.

part eight
Bibliography

This bibliography is a restricted one. The first set of references for each part are those which have been used in the book. These references have been numbered in the sequence in which they are mentioned in each part of the book.

Additional references have been included in each part to assist readers who wish to explore other points of view. Again, we have restricted our references to those we feel are helpful.

Bibliography

Part One. Introduction

1. Barnard, Chester I., *The Functions of the Executive.* Cambridge, Mass.: Harvard University Press, 1956.
2. Sloan, Alfred P., *My Years with General Motors.* Garden City, N.Y.: Doubleday, 1964.
3. Cordiner, Ralph J., *New Frontiers for Professional Managers.* New York: McGraw-Hill, 1956.
4. Maynard, H. B., editor, *Top Management Handbook.* New York: McGraw-Hill, 1960.
5. Allen, Louis A., *Management and Organization.* New York: McGraw-Hill, 1958.
   Allen, Louis A., *The Management Profession.* New York: McGraw-Hill, 1964.
6. Drucker, Peter, *Management.* New York: Harper & Row, 1974.

Drucker, Peter, *The Practice of Management.* New York: Harper & Row, 1954.
7. Dale, Ernest, *Planning and Developing the Company Organization Structure.* New York: American Management Association, 1952.
   Dale, Ernest, *The Great Organizers.* New York: McGraw-Hill, 1960.
8. Koontz, Harold, and Cyril O'Donnell, *Principles of Management.* New York: McGraw-Hill, 1972.
9. Newman, William H., *Administrative Action.* Englewood Cliffs, N.J.: Prentice-Hall, 1951.
10. Simon, Herbert A., *Administrative Behavior.* New York: Macmillan, 1947.
11. Holden, Paul E., Lounsbury S. Fish, and Herbert L. Smith, *Top Management Or-*

ganization and Control. Copyright 1951 McGraw-Hill Book Company.

12. Holden, Paul E., Carlton A. Pederson, and Gayton E. Germane, *Top Management.* McGraw-Hill, 1968. Used with permission of McGraw-Hill Book Company.

13. Newman, *Administrative Action.*

OTHER REFERENCES

Gross, Bertram M., *The Management of Organizations*, vol. 2. New York: Free Press of Glencoe, 1964.

Brown, Wilfred, *Explanation in Management.* London: Heinemann, 1960. The organizational structure, procedures, and philosophy of Glacier Metal Company of London, as presented by its chairman and managing director.

Part Two. Structure

1. Allen, Louis A., *Management and Organization.* New York: McGraw-Hill, 1958, p. 57.

2. Brown, Alvin, *Organization, a Formulation of Principle.* New York: Hibbert, 1945, p. 6.

3. Allen, *Management and Organization*, pp. 62–70. Used with permission of McGraw-Hill Book Company.

OTHER REFERENCES

Ansoff, H. I., and John M. Stewart, "Strategies for a Tech-nology-based Business," *Harvard Business Review*, November–December, 1967.

Buchele, Robert B., *Business Policy in Growing Firms.* San Francisco: Chandler, 1967.

Chandler, Alfred D., Jr., *Strategy and Structure.* Cambridge, Mass.: M.I.T. Press, 1962.

Carey, E. Raymond, and Steven H. Star, *Organization Strategy: A Marketing Approach.* Division of Research, Graduate School of Business Administration, Harvard University, 1971.

Goggin, William C., "How the Multi-dimensional Structure Works at Dow Corning," *Harvard Business Review*, January–February, 1974.

Guth, William, *Organizational Strategy: Analysis, Commitment, Implementation.* Homewood, Ill.: Richard D. Irwin, 1974.

Sayles, Leonard R., and Margaret K. Chandler, *Managing Large Systems: Organizations for the Future.* New York: Harper & Row, 1971.

Scott, Bruce R. "The Industrial State: Old Myths and New Realities," *Harvard Business Review*, March–April 1973.

Part Three. Power

1. Smith, George Albert, Jr., *Managing Geographically Decentralized Companies.* Cambridge, Mass.: Harvard University Press, 1958.

2. McGregor, Douglas. *The Professional Manager.* Copyright

1967 McGraw-Hill Book Company. Used with permission of McGraw-Hill Book Company.

3. Drucker, Peter, *Management.* New York: Harper & Row, 1974.

4. Zaleznick, Abraham, "Power and Politics in Organizational Life," *Harvard Business Review,* May–June, 1970, pp. 47–60.

5. Martin, Norman, and John Howard Sims, "Power Tactics," *Harvard Business Review,* November–December, 1956, pp. 25–29.

6. There is a voluminous literature on Organization Development. The following references have proven useful to managers:

Beckhard, Richard, *Organizational Development, Strategies, and Models.* Reading, Mass.: Addison-Wesley, 1969.

Bennis, W. G., K. D. Benne, and R. Chin editors, *The Planning of Change* (2nd edition). New York: Holt, Rinehart and Winston, 1969.

7 Allen, Louis A., *Management and Organization.* Copyright 1958 McGraw-Hill Book Company. Used with permission of McGraw-Hill Book Company.

8. Dearden, John, "Limits on Decentralized Profit Responsibility," *Harvard Business Review,* November–December, 1961, p. 87.

OTHER REFERENCES

Cleland, David I., and Wallace Munsey, "Who Works with Whom," *Harvard Business Review,* September–October, 1967.

Dalton, Melville, *Men Who Manage.* New York: John Wiley, 1959.

Gross, Bertram, M., *The Management of Organizations, vol. 1.* New York: Free Press of Glencoe, 1964.

Etzioni, Amitai, *Complex Organizations.* New York: Holt, Rinehart, and Winston, 1961.

Follett, Mary P., *Dynamic Administration.* New York: Harper, 1942.

Tannebaum, Arnold S., Bogdan Kavcic, Menachem Rosner, Mino Vianello, and George Wieser, *Hierarchy in Organizations.* San Francisco: Jossey-Bass, 1974.

Winter, David G., *The Power Motive.* Riverside, N.J.: The Free Press, 1973.

Part Four. Job Design

1. Drucker, Peter, *Management.* New York: Harper & Row, 1974, pp. 403–18.

2. Lutz, Carl F., and Albert P. Ingraham, "Design and Management of Positions," *Personnel Journal,* April 1972, pp. 236–37.

3. Drucker, Peter, *Management,* pp. 405–10.

OTHER REFERENCES

Nadler, Gerald, *Work Design*, Homewood, Ill.: Richard D. Irwin, 1963.

Part Five. Staffing

1. Allen, Louis A., *The Management Profession*. New York: McGraw-Hill, 1964, pp. 287–89.
2. Mahler, Walter R., and William F. Wrightnour, *Executive Continuity*. Homewood, Ill.: Dow Jones–Irwin, 1974.

Part Seven. Special Issues

1. National Industrial Conference Board, *Top Management Organization in Divisionalized Companies*. Studies in Personnel Policy, no. 195, 1965.

OTHER REFERENCES

Bower, Marvin, *The Will to Manage*. New York: McGraw-Hill, 1966.

Clee, G. H., and Wilbur M. Sachtgen, "Organizing a Worldwide Business," *Harvard Business Review*, November–December 1964.

Greiner, Larry E., "Evolution and Revolution as Organizations Grow," *Harvard Business Review*, July–August 1972.

Muller-Thym, B. J., "Practices in General Management, New Directions for Organizational Practices," *ASME Journal of Engineering for Industry*, 1960.

Index

Index